Dr. Dreck's B Movie Museum

DR DRECKS

B MOVIE MUSEUM

Dedicated to:

Ed McDonnell

Portrayer of "Feep" of Fantasmic Features

out of Boston, MA

My first horror host

and to

Lorna Nogueira, who has been with me since

the start of the show

ACKNOWLEDGMENTS

There's always lots of people to acknowledge, isn't there? Your influences, mentors, friends, family, etc.

I would first acknowledge Scary Monsters magazine, which gave me the idea of becoming a horror host to begin with. I was reading articles about other like minded weirdos breaking into public access stations and using public domain films for their shows. I thought it looked like fun. "I think I'll do that for a few years," I said to myself. At this writing it's been eleven years, and we haven't stopped yet.

I am so appreciative of the Forgotten Horrors series of books by Michael Price, George Turner and John Wooley. They have made me aware of so many obscure little B movie gems that I've subsequently used on my show. They, like me, are not fond of the "snark" generation, and think the films deserve much more respect than they get.

I purposely did a more retro show than most of the new horror hosts. In  other words, I don't insert myself into the movie or make comments while it's running. The movie speaks for itself; if you want to sit there and make fun of it, be my guest, at least I don't have to hear you. I'm very fond of these movies; I enjoy them for they are.

I don't do the show alone. I have a wonderful bunch of loons who appear with me. So thank you to Roberta Marsden, Diane Mela, Robert Legge, Dwight Kemper and especially my adorable Lorna Nogueira, who makes for an adorable zombie. I can't forget Stu, Shrunken Ed, Williard, Bigfoot, Mr. Maniac or Arthur, either.

And to my horror host brethren, past and present, thanks to you, too, for keeping this very weird niche of entertainment open and alive.

FORWARD

Michael Legge offers hope for the dwindling craft of responsible film criticism. His Dr. Dreck commentaries make no bones about the intrinsic raggedness of his chosen idiom, the chump-change horror-fantasy pictures—nor does he offer any apologies for the preference. The cowardly and infantile notion of the Guilty Pleasure is nowhere to be found, here. Fresh air, in other words, in a field long since polluted by the Snark Merchants who wouldn't know a Thoughtful Appraisal if it bit them. Legge knows from Thoughtful Appraisals, and he dispenses them generously in these playful and conversational essays. He also derives no end of delight from the act of passing along such enthusiasm, to the exclusion of Egghcad Ivory Tower Film Theorism. Not that there's anything wrong with Film Theorism. I've been practicing that approach since the early days of the American Film Institute, which enlisted my mentor, George E. Turner, and me around 1968 to help compile empirical, primary-source studies of any number of films for the project that became The A.F.I. Catalogue of Motion Pictures. George and I found ourselves responsible for the Poverty Row titles, for the most part:"So you chaps drew the short straw," said an Ivory Tower Egghead colleague, Bill Everson at N.Y.U., who preferred the major-studio pictures. No short-straw nonsense for George and me: Our A.F.I. research turned into the Forgotten Horrors series, which since 1979 has become the longest-running film-history franchise in commercial publishing. Ten volumes and counting, anyhow. So there, already.And that success stems primarily (or so I believe) from our willingness to take these stepchild movies as earnestly as we would any bigger picture from Universal, or Paramount, or RKO, or—yes, well, you get the idea. Meanwhile, the broader mass-media field of film reviewing has been overrun by the celebrity-gossip hacks and the snarkheads who will trash a picture even if they happen to dig it. Lemmings.

All of which can only make Michael Legge's observations all the more refreshing. Not to mention, meaningful. A welcome addition to the genre-study field, yet.

—Michael H. Price
Lead author
Forgotten Horrors et Seq.

A WORD FROM MOANER

Um, hello. Moaner Johnson here. Co-host, zombie and proud denizen of the Dungeon of Dr. Dreck. Dr. Dreck has asked me to write a little foreword for his new book celebrating B movies. I am happy to do so. I remember when I was a little eleven year old zombie, watching something called The Creature Double Feature. It was broadcast on a local UHF station on Saturday afternoons. My little monster friends and I would watch the horror and sci-fi movies then go out and try to terrify each other with playful reenactments of them. B-movies do capture and stimulate our imaginations and it's only fitting that someone take notice.

When he was a boy-mad-doctor-in-the-making, Dr. Dreck lived and breathed these movies and his genuine fondness for them makes him the perfect candidate to showcase them. He knows way more than anyone should about them, all the entertaining minutiae and players in the genre. As a cheerleader, albeit a dead one, I have nothing on Dr. Dreck when it comes to championing the work of the obscure and neglected. Movies are hard to make but even people who are not millionaires want to make them. Filmmakers come in all shapes, sizes, creeds and economic strata and Dr. Dreck recognizes bright lights when he sees them.

Yes, B-movies have flaws and thank goodness. Perfection is predictable and boring! Art is a bumpy, messy road - a fact Dr. Dreck understands.

I write this foreword with one caveat: while I mostly defer to Dr. Dreck in terms of movie lore, I strongly contest his claim that crooner-heartthrob Page Cavanaugh was not in every horror film we have shown on our public access program. (See page '109') Even if you don't always see him, my dreamboat Page is there in spirit. As far as I'm concerned every film, ever, should feature a

Page Cavanaugh ditty.   Bones of contention aside, please peruse and enjoy this book by my esteemed, smarty pants colleague, Dr. Dreck.

WHAT'S SO BAD ABOUT BAD?

Back in the late 70's, a smug, condescending book came out titled, The 50 Worst Movies of All Time. It was later followed by the Golden Turkey awards. These books paved the way for the MST3K crowd of snarky hipsters who think they're cool when they're trashing something. I will say something unpopular here; I do not like MST3K. As far as I'm concerned they are parasites, living off others people's work. They also trash movies that really aren't that bad, some of which I defend in this book, and they really crossed the line when they attacked This Island Earth, a true 50's classic. Their defenders say, "But they really like these movies!" Oh yeah? That's like saying, "My wife is fat, stupid and ugly, but I LOVE HER!" I've watched some of the shows, and all I can hear is a sneering contempt for what they show. Let me be clear, there are no BAD movies. There are movies that may be bad to you or to me, but those same movies may be loved by others.

Even if they're loved for being bad, in my book the love negates the "badness". It's all so subjective. Many people will argue about whether an actor is good or bad, and both are right, but in their own mind. You can't tell me an actor is bad if I don't think so, and vice versa. Have I ever seen a movie I consider bad? Of course. Bad to me. For me, there is one single element that makes a movie bad to me, and that's the story. If the story is boring, pointless and lacking any heart or depth, then it doesn't matter how much money is put into it, or if it has the best director or biggest stars. It will still be bad to me. On the other hand, I've seen low budget movies with adequate acting and directing, but with an interesting story. That's not a bad movie, it's a movie without enough resources. Many a cheap movie cleverly overcome their threadbare budgets. For example, in *The Brain that Wouldn't Die*, a car crash is creatively done through editing, and with the use of car door window with a fire burning in front of the lens. Say what you will about the movie itself, that's damn smart. So we come to B movies, which also takes in a lot of the public domain movies floating around out there. B movies came into being as the second feature accompanying the "A" feature. It was a budget picture, made very quickly, and in a recognizable genre. They were usually short; some just shy of an hour, the longer ones going to 75 minutes. They were the pulp fiction of movies. High adventure, outlandish plots, murders, car chases, aliens, monsters in caves, kidnapped women, sub human beasts, you name it. They could take place in the jungle, a city, the lonely countryside, an old dark house, the prairie, or another planet. A lot of them were fun, escapist entertainment, while others were boring, being mostly talk. Before the Disney Corporation lobbyists helped to buy off congress so as to extend copyrights, movies had a life span of 56 years at most. An initial 28 years, (in which the copyright notice had to be visible and correct in the film's credits, and the movie had to be registered in the Library of Congress), then it could be renewed for another 28 years. If the company didn't renew, the movie fell into public domain. In any case the movie would fall into public domain after 56 years. Now that law changed in the late 70's, so it no longer holds true. Presently, it's 95 years from the date issued. This is why the Karloff classic, Frankenstein, is still under copyright. Before the new law, it would be in PD now. Consequently, no movies are falling into PD recently and won't be for a long time. The movies that are in PD now, go back to the 20's into the 60's. Some of the movies were registered but didn't include the copyright notice in the films credits. They became PD when they were first screened. Not so now. What has happened to some extent is that these PD movies have become the fodder of the movie trash patrol. They're old, they're in black and white, the prints are usually battered, and the sound is tinny so they've just got to be bad, right? We don't really need to look at them, just ridicule them. Take this test. Think of two or three of your favorite movies, then go the Amazon customer reviews of that movie and find the people that give that movie one star. They hate it and they always say the same lame things; bad acting, bad story, bad directing, bad photography, etc, like they know everything there is to know about making movies. So do you say to yourself, "My god, they're right! What a fool I've been! It must be bad!" Of course not, even if most of the customer ratings are below 2 stars, you still love that movie, they won't change your mind. They're the idiots, not you. So what I'm saying? I don't know. You tell me. Oh, yeah, I think what I'm trying to say is USE YOUR BRAIN. Don't let robot jerks with big mouths tell you what to like or not like. In this book, I am reviewing movies that I've shown on my program, The Dungeon of Dr. Dreck. If you're expecting me to give glowing reviews of all of them, you'd be wrong. If you expect to learn new trivia and facts about the movies, you're out of luck. This is my personal memoir, if you will, and everything is seen through my own unique magnifying glass. If you expect some humor, you'd be right. But I give these movies a fair shake. I'm prejudiced, I know. I grew up seeing and loving these movies as a kid, but I can still see the merit in most of them; even the worst of them. So, come along, leave your preconceptions and cheese detector behind, and we'll explore my B movie museum. Please note that I will not give detailed synopsis of each movie. Plot summaries are easy to find anywhere, and I always skip them when I'm reading a book about movies. SPOILERS ARE INCLUDED SO WATCH YOUR STEP! My point of view in the comments are light hearted and meant to be fun. I love these movies for what they are, and hope whomever reads this feels the same way.

VOODOO MAN

Bela once again makes bad decisions as he kidnaps young women to transfer their life essence to his wife.

The very first movie I showed on my program is one of the infamous "Monogram Nine" which sounds more like a criminal trial than a series of low budget pictures. Bela Lugosi, whose talent was ignored by the studio that he helped made famous through his classic portrayal of Dracula, found he could still be a star in a small studio. Monogram was a poverty row studio, who along with PRC Studios occupied the bottom tier of Hollywood studios in terms of prestige. However, these scruffy little studios still managed to turn out some interesting, moody, and even iconic movies. In Voodoo Man, Lugosi is enacting one of the tried and true plots of horror films, restoring his wife to the land of the living. She is currently in a zombie like state, and while nice to look at, is rather inadequate in two way conversations. Bela's solution is to kidnap young women and transfer their life spark to her via some weird voodoo god called Ramboona. He is assisted by John Carradine and George Zucco, and this is the only picture they ever appeared in together. (They almost appeared together in Return of the Ape Man, but as production started George had the good sense to become ill and bow out. There is a production photo of George in his ape man get up, and it's no wonder he got sick.) However, George still had to stifle his dignity to appear in his voodoo get up, sporting war paint and feathers. Bad enough he had to run a gas station, let alone look like a berserk turkey. As always, he took it seriously as he chanted and threw spells left and right, always insisting that "Ramboona never fails," even though Ramboona never succeeds in this movie. John Carradine seems to be having a grand time, playing a half wit assistant, as he jogs around, his hair in his face, and admiring the pretty girls Bela keeps lined up in see through cabinets. Carradine was stashing his money away for his Shakespeare company, so he would take any job at this point.

Directed by William Beaudine, this is quite a fun bit of balderdash, and Lugosi gives it his customary full throttle performance, much to his credit.

FRANKENSTEIN'S DAUGHTER

Oliver Frankenstein, a descendent of you know who, creates a female monster in between hitting on every woman who comes within ten feet of him.

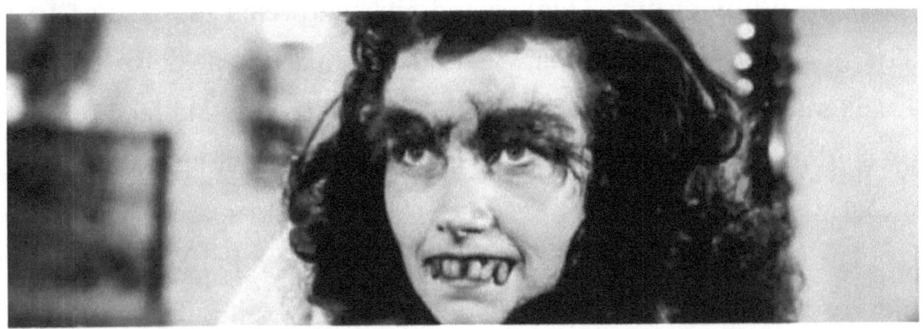

I so love this movie. Richard Cunha outdid himself with this incredibly wacky, sleazy, gory variation on the Frankenstein legend.   Sandra Knight is not the daughter, except for a few minutes when Oliver Frankenstein, (that's right, "Oliver"), slips her a monster mickey, and she gets all ugly and hairy, running up and down the street in her bathing suit and robe. The real "daughter" could be considered a transgender monster. The make up artist, Harry Thomas, thought the monster to be a male and made him up accordingly. At the last minute when it was too late, he found out the monster was supposed to be female, so all he could do was slap some lipstick on the beast.   Made all the difference in the world, don't you think? What I get a kick of is actor Donald Murphy, who looks to me like Ward Cleaver's evil twin. He is so over the top loony and egotistical, that he should run for Congress where he would fit in nicely. The music highlight is two fold.   Page Cavanaugh's Trio performs the musical ditty, "Special Date," and then Harold Lloyd, Jr. bounces his way through "Daddy Bird." (Adapted from Beethoven's Sonata of the same name.) We had a running gag on the show where Moaner fell in love with Page Cavanaugh, who looks like he wandered in from an Ozzie and Harriet show. I didn't know until later, that he actually had a long career as a respected jazz musician, and cut many albums. When he died I felt genuinely sad, since we had had so much fun with him. Unexpected gore surprised me when I first saw this movie.   A man gets squashed in a door by the Frankenfemale and spits up blood, and Oliver gets his face burned by acid in the finale. It still grosses me out, even though I know the effect was done with lens paper and chocolate syrup.

The most amazing performance is given by Felix Locher, the elderly gent with the accent. I've seen him in other TV show and movies, but he's always had a bit part. He has a large part in this one, and his performance is interesting. When Oliver tries to kill him or threatens him, he gets momentarily miffed, then shrugs it off. Maybe he was used to having his life threatened, I don't know, but his stiff delivery of lines and reactions to the outrageous events is really awe inspiring. Everyone must have been aware of what a goofy movie they were 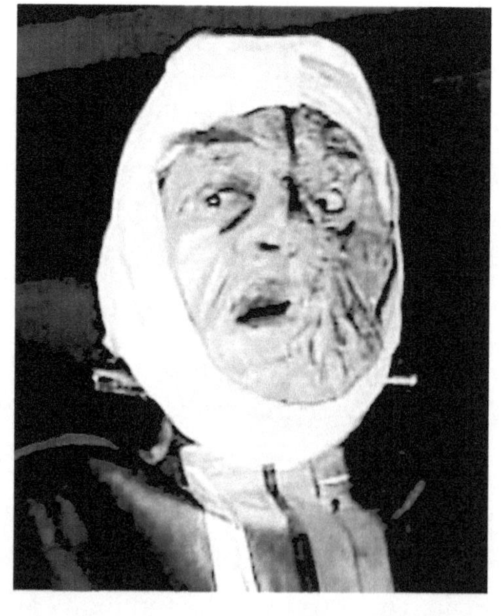 making, (except maybe Felix), at least I hope so, because they are all fun to watch.   John Ashley is the nominal hero, and he's his usual dull self, but at least he doesn't sing. Sandra Knight ended up as Jack NIcholson's first wife, which was probably harder than making this movie.

BRAIN THAT WOULDN'T DIE

When the fiancé of a doctor is decapitated in an auto accident, he grabs the head, brings it home, puts it in a chemical tray and tries to find a new body to attach the head to. I don't think this is in the Hippocratic Oath.

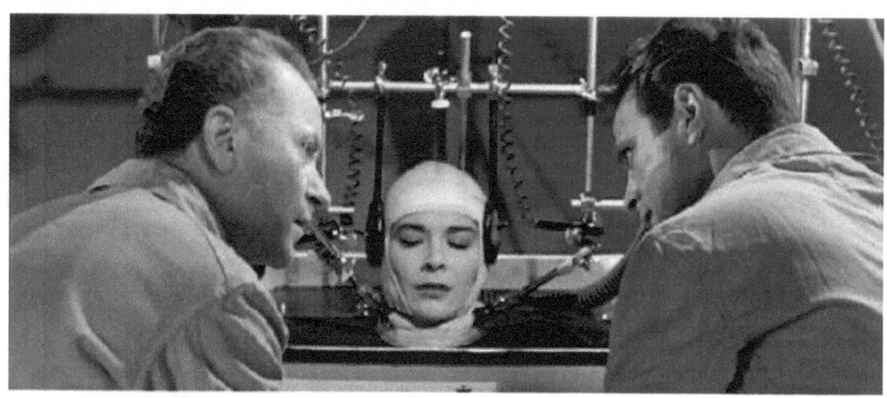

During this time period, (the 50's, early 60's), there was a slew of living head movies. This is the most outrageous and the most fun. Boy loves girl. Girl loses head. Boy takes head. Boy tries to get new body for head. Arm gets pulled off. Giant goon comes out of closet, literally not figuratively. They should have given out an Oscar for the best performance by a head. I think that Virginia Leith should have walked away with it, or just being a head, rolled away with it. At the beginning she is a mature, sexy woman, but she spends most of her time up to her neck in a metal tray, and she makes the most of it. She chose to have a raspy voice, which is quite unsettling, and her venom and outrage is palpable, no matter what bizarre dialog she has to spout out. She also has one of the most chilling laughs I've ever heard. Sleazy, cheap, and gory are just a few words used to describe this movie, which to my knowledge was actually shot in the late 50's but didn't get released till the early 60s. As I said in the introduction, the movie does make use of its limited resources, and the car crash is done very effectively. The supremo gory scene, of course, is when the lab assistant, Kurt, gets his arm pulled off by the monster.   He

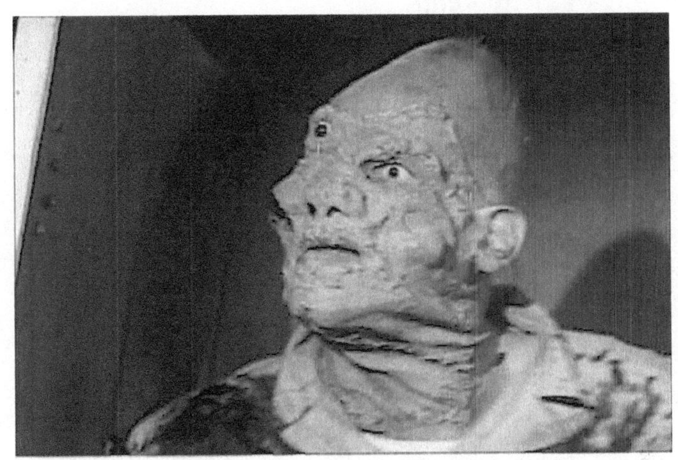

stumbles around the lab smearing blood on the walls, makes his way upstairs but I guess he needed that particular arm to dial the phone, so he goes all the way back downstairs, stumbles around a little more and finally dies. The only other person I can remember who took that long to die was Basil Rathbone in *A Comedy of Terrors*, but that was meant to be funny. I think if Kurt could have focused his energy, he could have walked to the nearest hospital in all that time. He's not the only guy to get messy, though. Jason Evers, the sleazy doctor looking for the most beautiful body he can find to replace the "from the neck down" department of his fiancé, gets to have his neck chomped by super Zippy the pinhead from the closet. Zippy dangles the bloody piece of meat for the camera and throws it on the floor. Now that he's free and the place is on fire, he wisely decides to take the latest female victim with him. She's unconscious so she doesn't mind. The head laughs to the end credits. You may laugh too, but you never know. Your head may end up in a tray someday.

ROBOT MONSTER

A little boy has a nightmare which turns into one of the funniest movies every made.

This movie has the reputation of being one of the most fun bad movies ever made but is it really all that bad? Consider this. The humorous parts of this movie are undeniable; the ridiculous monster of the title, the bubble machine that Lawrence Welk would have envied, the strange dialogue between a lot of principal players and the killing of the little girl which was very odd at the time this movie was made. But what a lot of people fail to take into consideration is that the movie is actually the dream of the little boy. Do you remember when you were a little kid? How much sense did your dreams make? How many laughable aspects were there when you woke up and thought about it? Since this boy is growing up in the 50s, he probably watches the TV shows of the time. Maybe his favorites were Sea Hunt and Jungle Jim. In his dream, symbols from the shows get scrambled into the dream monster. The diving helmet is from Sea Hunt, and the body of the gorilla from Jungle Jim. Why not? Most little boys love dinosaurs, too, so let's throw them into the dream stew. Now I know the director never intended this, at least I don't think he did, but even so, if you look at it knowing it's a little kids' dream, it makes more sense. He could have been pissed off at this sister too, so he kills her in his dream. He doesn't know much about love and marriage, hence the silly romantic interplay and wedding between the adults.

If we can cut slack for the short comings of *Invaders from Mars* which is also a child's dream, maybe we can do the same for *Robot Monster.*

It's pretty impossible to sit through this movie without laughing or at least smiling. It's so joyously goofy that you can't get mad at it for being so cheesy. When I first showed this movie, I think I was too hard on it. Now, after multiple viewings, I think it's some kind of unintentional surreal masterpiece.

As a side note, director Tucker also helmed the film, *Dance Hall Racket*, which starred Lenny Bruce!

One of the biggest pleasures of my childhood during the 50's and 60's was going to the movies, but even though I went to plenty of indoor movies, I really loved the drive in theaters. During that time, there were three drive in theaters in my part of central Massachusetts. There was one right in my home town of Mendon, but also the Quaker Drive In of Uxbridge, and the Bellingham Auto Theater. The last two are long gone, but the good old Mendon Drive In is still there doing thriving business. I can remember so many of the fun horror and science fiction movies I saw at these "ozoners." *The Mysterians, Blood of Dracula, Kronos, 20 Million Miles to Earth, Three Stooges Meet Hercules, The Reptile, Dracula Has Risen From the Grave, Plague of the Zombies, Godzilla, Psycho;* the list goes on and on. This was before the lawsuit happy days when there were playgrounds at the theater. The unhealthy food was there too, of course, but that was one of the pleasures as well. I recently visited the Mendon Drive In and had fried dill pickles which I didn't think I'd like, but I did! During my youngest years, stashed in the backseat of the car with my brother, I did fall asleep a lot. I still remember seeing the credits open to the original *The Fly*. The next thing I remember is the car engine starting up to head for home. My family had to describe the movie to me and it wasn't until much later that I finally saw the film on TV. When we started the Dr. Dreck show, I paid homage to the deceased drive ins, showing footage I took of the ruins of them, with the screens still standing

amidst overgrown weeds and debris. The gang at the dungeon made their own "pretend" drive in, and we sat at different tables with old car facades in front of us. Groaner ran a snack bar a few feet away from us. Madame Nicotina, Shrunken Ed, Stu and later Williard were there in their separate cars. We showed a cartoon, a trailer and one movie, (no double feature, sorry), and tried to relive the fun and excitement of the experience. A few years later we went further and produced a real drive in atmosphere with all the appropriate surroundings and sound ambience.I tried to pick typical drive in type movies, usually science fiction, since that was the biggest thing during the 50s and 60s, but some horror snuck in there as well. These shows are the most fun to me, because the entire cast appeared and interacted.The drive in will always bring a nostalgic glow to me. I imagine myself at six years old, both of my parents still alive, and me half asleep in the back seat, feeling the rumble of the family car as we headed home.

BRIDE OF THE GORILLA

Raymond Burr goes ape over Barbara Payton.

Curt Siodmak wrote and directed this knockoff of *The Wolf Man*, with the main cast famous for different reasons. In the original script Siodmak intended to have the cursed man see himself as a gorilla subjectively. He wanted to have the point of view of the gorilla, to give the impression that it was a delusion rather than a reality. (I understand he wanted to do this in the original script of the Wolf Man as well. No real monster fan wants to be deprived of their monster so cooler heads prevailed at Universal and we got to see Lon Chaney in all his hairy glory.) Through most of the movie, the point of view is Raymond Burr's which would make you think that he is imagining his transformation, but the movie gives it away with an objective view of the gorilla so unless the audience also has a gorilla fixation the transformation in the movie is real.   Raymond Burr plays the gorilla man with all the intensity he had shown in his film noir roles. Of course, soon afterwards, he became the iconic good guy as Perry Mason. (I like him in the American version of Godzilla, critics be damned.) Lon Chaney has a good guy role for a change. He does what he can with a role that is fairly perfunctory and as he was a "friend" of Siodmak, that may be how he got into this. (From what I've read, having Siodmak as a friend, meant you didn't need any enemies.   He trashed Lon and others in interviews.) It's always fun to see Lon anyway, especially when he still looks in decent shape.

Barbara Payton, the Va Va Voom blonde in the picture, was a well known party girl, who sadly drank her way into oblivion and ended up as a prostitute.

RAYMOND BURR ON THE EDGE OF IMMORTALITY AS PERRY MASON. BARBARA PAYTON ON THE EDGE OF FAME BEFORE FALLING OFF INTO OBLIVION.

THE CRAWLING EYE

Aliens camp out on top of a mountain and kill time by ripping the heads off people.

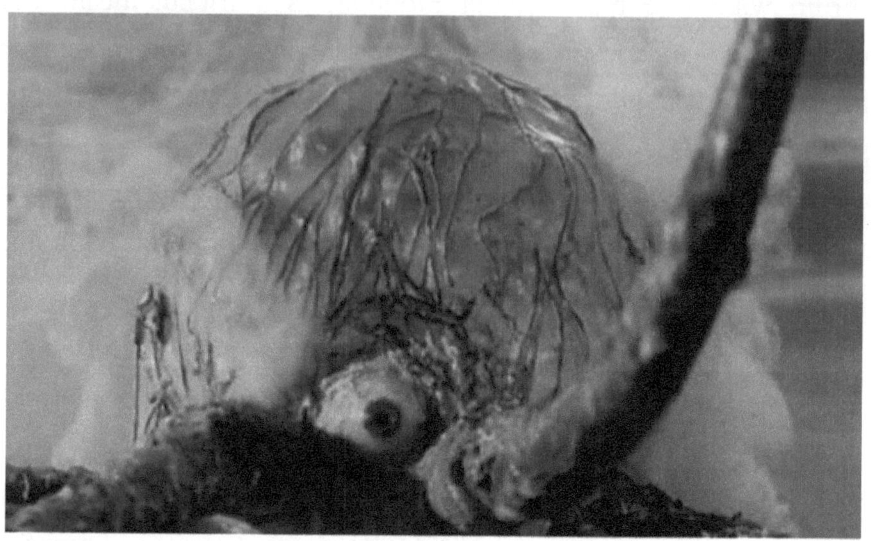

The first I knew of his film was as a little boy, seeing the newspaper ad. It was of a human eye with tentacles coming out of it. Scared me silly. My brother went to see it with my dad, and he told me about the infamous severed head in a bag. It wasn't until many years later that I got to see it. This movie really has a lot going for it. It seems like a Nigel Kneale script, which is probably what they were going for, since the Quatermass series was very successful then. Jimmy Sangster does a very good job with his story. Like the Brit sci-fi pictures of the day, they got an American actor to head the cast, to give it more oomph for US audiences. Forrest Tucker takes the role. At the time I saw it, I only knew him from *F Troop*, so it was weird for me at the time to see him in a serious role, although he carries it off nicely. (Kind of like people who know Leslie Neilson from *Police Squad*, and then see one of the serious roles he did previously.) Janet Munro is also effective as the psychic. I must make special mention of Andrew Faulds, who plays the possessed "dead" man who comes down from the mountain. His inability to coordinate his motions because he is being manipulated like a puppet is very effective and chilling. And that look on his face. Stay away from me, please. As for the crawling eyes, they are most effective when you see a large icky

eye looking through the door way, and when the tentacles come slithering in the room. Shades of Lovecraft. We see their full bodies on a miniature set, sitting on top of the building. Now here's where people like to ridicule it. But I look at it this way. You know you're watching a low budget movie. They can't afford animatronic or stop motion effects, so they make these little puppet monsters. But I don't care. I like them for what they are. The only detraction might be is that they're kind of cute. But they're really "there." They were made with some ingenuity and manipulated by human hands. You see a CGI effect nowadays, and you may be dazzled, but with the preponderance of them, they become soulless. Hell, half the time that you're seeing the actors, they're really being green screened; they're not even really there. I've seen actors green screened to simply do a walk down the street shot. I'll take real any day.

PLAN 9 FROM OUTER SPACE

The question will always be: What were the other eight plans?

What can you say about Plan 9 that hasn't been said? Is it the worst movie ever made? No. There is no worst movie ever made, because everyone has a different opinion about which movie that is. Plan 9 is not boring; it's fun, it's not slick, it's disarmingly cheap, it's not badly written, it's written in Woodese, a language that requires a college course to fully understand.

I first saw this movie on TV sometime in the mid 60's. At the time it was just an elusive, lost Lugosi movie that I wanted to see. I did get to see poor old Bela, for about four minutes. I didn't know at the time that his footage was shot previously for some future Wood epic. Then I got to see him again, coming in and out of the forest to flourish his cape for no apparent reason. I could see the stand-in was not Bela; I was young, but not that gullible. I also knew Tor Johnson, from Black Sleep and others. At the time I didn't know I was seeing a "bad" movie. I liked seeing flying saucers and Tor and flashes of Lugosi. It was the first time I saw Vampira other than in a photograph. The two most effective scenes to me were with her and Tor. Tor had cornered the market on blank staring eyes and open mouth grimace, and Vampira looked like she was struggling with rigor mortis in her role. Together when they were trudging around was actually pretty creepy. The other creepy moment was when the resurrected Tor climbed out of the grave, fiendishly lit from below. This being an Ed Wood movie, you wonder if a light accidentally fell into the hole and Wood said, "Ah, leave it and shoot it anyway. It looks kind of cool." Accident or not, it is quite ghoulish looking.

The aliens, all of three of them, seem kind of harmless to me; Dudley Manlove with his rich announcer tones, and his hapless female assistant, Joanna Lee. The big boss, John Breckenridge, seems bored with the whole thing. Lyle Talbot adds the most class

to it, probably wishing he were talking over the fence to Ozzie Nelson rather than being stuck in this. However, he'd been in three Wood films, so I think the paycheck was doing the talking. He also narrated the atrocious *Mesa of Lost Women,* which may be worse than a Ed Wood movie.

I never get tired of seeing Plan 9, and that makes it a good movie to me. It's so out there and fascinating, I wish it had a been a big hit and Wood made a lot more movies like it. But with a low budget. Lots of money would have spoiled Ed's style.

THE CREEPING TERROR

A people eating carpet lands on Earth and steals the soundtrack to this movie.

Even the worst of so called bad movies may have some redeeming feature. This seems to be the exception. I still remember the first time I saw this one; my jaw dropped open and stayed that way. Caught a lot of flies. This notorious movie was put together initially by star Vic Savage, who corralled some investors into putting up dough for his movie. There are conflicting stories about why there is no live dialog soundtrack. Some say it was never recorded live on location; others say it was lost, stolen or was grabbed by Savage as he headed for the hills and left everyone holding the bag. At any rate, we have a movie that is mostly narrated, has a terribly cheap monster made of what looks like carpet fragments and other junk, and lacked a competent film editor who let scenes drag on forever. The movie could have been better than it is. Just having a live soundtrack with dialog would have helped. Coming up with a better looking monster would have been a big plus as well, although it does show a certain amount of creativity in its design. In long shots, it sort of looks likes a small brontosaurus. Perhaps if they didn't show it for any length of time it would have helped, or had night time attacks only, obscuring the monster with deep shadows. A common idiocy of a lot of movies, both old and new, is of the victim who instead of running away, just stands there and screams, or worse, faints while the monster takes it sweet time coming to get them. This movie doubles down on that cliche. The victims have to actively climb into the mouth of the monster to be eaten. I'm surprised they didn't sprinkle salt on themselves on the way in to make themselves more palatable to the creature.

Yes, this movie could have been a lot better, but I don't see how it could have been worse.

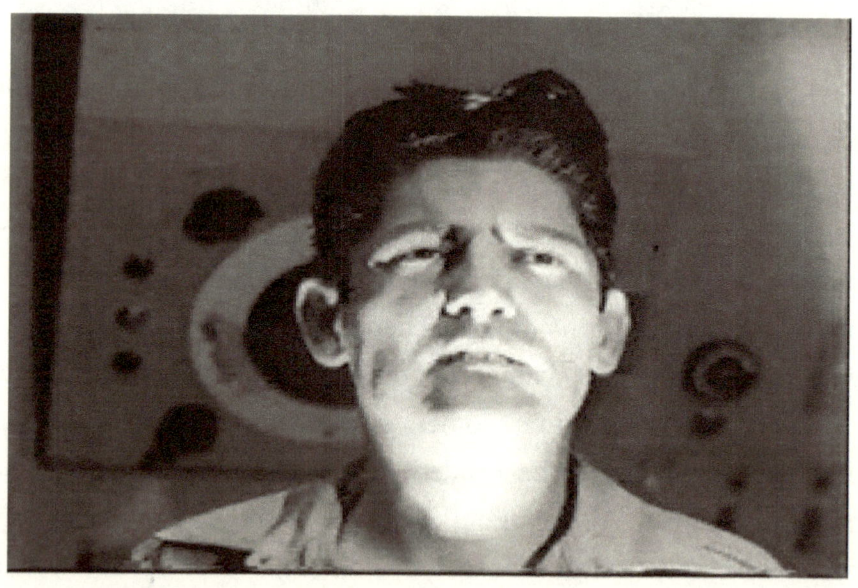

"YOU KNOW, I DON'T THINK I WANT TO FINISH THIS MOVIE...

THE BRAINIAC

An alien monster has a strict diet. He can only eat human brains.

When a slew of Mexican horror films first hit TV during the 60's, I was not all that interested. But hey, I was young, and I didn't appreciate a lot of things back then. Now, I love these Mexican weird fests. Even though people slam American distributer K. Gordon Murray for the lousy dubbing, he brought them to our attention, and for that I'm eternally grateful to him. Mexican horror films are like nothing else. They are kind of like a cinematic piñata. A garish looking thing swinging in front of you, but when you hit it just right, a lot of goodies fall out. The weirdest of all the Mexican movies I've seen is this one. Where else can you find a monster that not only sucks out people's brains with a long ant eater like appendage, but his head expands and contracts as well. He looks like some fairy tale monster; pointed ears, widows peak, long nose, a long beard, you name it.

The monster is played by Abel Salazar, who along with German Robles were like the Christopher Lee and Peter Cushing of Mexican horror. This time around, poor German is a victim instead of a predator, as he stares in a wide eyed trance waiting to have his brain turned into a Slurpy.

A special treat is seeing Salazar, in his human guise, take time out for a "brain" snack that he keeps in a cabinet. Mmmm, yummy.

German Robles as Count Lavud made a fabulous vampire in *El Vampiro*, and may have been the first screen bloodsucker to sport an impressive set of fangs. In that epic, Salazar was the hero who defeated the vampire. Imagine if we had both the Brainiac and Count Lavud in the same film!

Many of the Mexican horror flicks seem to be influenced to some extent by the Universal classics, in that they know how to generate an atmosphere and they love their monsters. As we all do.

Mexican movies live in a world different from ours, which I'll expound on later when I comment on one of the Santo movies.

"NOW I KNOW WHAT IT'S LIKE TO BE SUCKED INSTEAD OF DOING THE SUCKING."

THE DEVIL'S MESSENGER

Lon Chaney is the hardest working demon in hell.

Back in the 60's, Lon Chaney was the host of a TV horror anthology series called *13 Demon Street*, which although filmed in Sweden, was spoken in English. It was syndicated here for a brief time, with Lon opening and closing the show. As far as I know, it has never had a legitimate release on DVD, and the bootleg editions supposedly have a lot of Chaney's stuff cut out of them. (You would think this would be a selling point.) At any rate, three of these episodes were edited into this feature, the difference being that instead of hosting the stories, Chaney plays Satan in wraparound segments. While it's easy to imagine Vincent Price or John Carradine playing that part to the hilt, its kind of a kick to see Chaney's Satan, who seems more like a blue collar kind of guy, working in shirt sleeves in what must be a very stuffy office, otherwise known as the entrance to Hell. He's lucky his Rolodex doesn't burst into flame. He must be used to the heat as well, since he isn't sweating.

The stories are a mixed bag, the best one being The Photograph. This premise was used by M.R. James in a short story in which the figures in a painting keep moving around every time you look at them. The pilot film of *Night Gallery* used this device in the Roddy McDowell sequence. In this movie, it's a photograph that changes, in which a murdered woman approaches the viewer closer and closer. The next sequence is so-so; Girl in the Glacier is the weakest of the three. Condemned in Crystal is the longest one, and is quite good. Chaney enjoys being the devil, especially at the end when he has one of his minions deliver a formula to the human race for the ultimate bomb. Thing is, if humanity is wiped out, who's left for the Devil to claim? Maybe he'll put a sign on his door, "Gone Fission."

"THIS ROLODEX WILL SOON BE REPLACED BY A CELL PHONE; A TRUE DEVIL'S INSTRUMENT!"

CATWOMEN OF THE MOON

Astronauts discover a race of cat like women on the moon. Hilarity ensues.

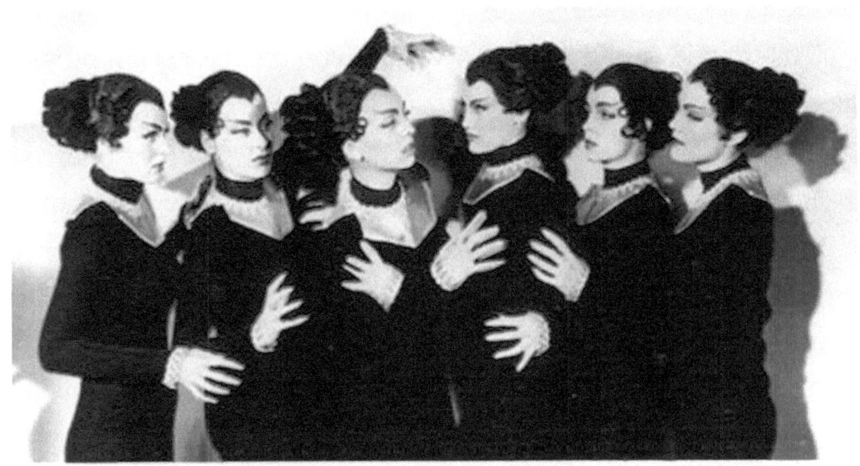

Here's one of those movies where the title itself becomes a joke. Along with the title *I Was a Teenage Werewolf*, (a great B movie no matter what anyone says), it came to epitomize the 50's sci-fi movie genre of outlandish premises. Other than in the way they look, how these are "cat" women is beyond me, since I never once see them clawing furniture or begging to be fed every five minutes. That's not like any cat I know. There was a bunch of male fantasy movies made during this period. (Like there isn't now, right?) There was *Queen of Outer Space, Missile to the Moon and Fire Maidens From Outer Space*. Even Abbott and Costello got into the act with an all female planet in *Go to Mars*. (Although, they're Venusians.)

I'm surprised no one has done a gay version of this one yet called Dog Men of the Moon. Or at least have all female astronauts land on a planet of all men. Victor Jory and Marie Windsor really deserved to be in a better movie than this, as both were fine character actors in other vehicles. It's a little weird to see Victor Jory as the male romantic lead instead of Sonny Tufts, but maybe Tufts needed less dialog to remember. He had alcohol problems and seemed to have a problem biting women's legs which got him into all kinds of trouble.

This movie was shot in 3D, which would have been a point of interest when it was first screened. However, even in 2D it's a lot of fun to watch.

Seems like the cat women's problem could have been solved with a little sensible negotiation with Earth. I think the men of Earth would welcome the boatload of lookers that were the Cat-Women.

This spider is like an old friend, she's been in so many cheap movies. I hope she at least got compensated for web use. She should have her own page on IMDB.

"HEY GUYS! HOW DO YOU LIKE
MY NEW HAT?"

LAST MAN ON EARTH

Vampires take over the earth and they can have it.

I've heard different gripes about this movie, but I still think this is the best adaptation I've seen of Richard Matheson's *I Am Legend*. Okay, I've only seen *Omega Man* and not the Will Smith reboot, and it's not I didn't like *Omega Man*, it just seemed further removed from the source material. One of the most common complaints is that Vincent Price is miscast. Why? Do people think it would always be a Joe Six Pack type that's the last man on earth? Why couldn't it be a cultured, sophisticated person like Vinnie? Actually, it must be more upsetting for someone like his character to have to do the things he has to do. I agree with anyone that says this was an inspiration to *Night of the Living Dead*. This and *Invisible Invaders* really seem to be precursors to that classic film. There are truly eerie sequences in this. Just the vampires, (who seem more like braindead zombies than vampires), attacking and pounding on the house all night long is enough to give me the heebie jeebies. Plus, the scene where he sees his dead wife in the door way after being freshly buried, is a real chiller. I like the matter of fact way Price goes through his daily routine, demonstrating that human beings can get used to anything in order to survive. It's especially poignant when he breaks down watching old home movies. It's also heartbreaking when he has to kill the dog that is infected, although if it were me, I'd keep the dog around to see what happened. How would a vampire dog behave? If Price's character is immune to the disease, then even if the dog bit him, he'd be safe. Just give the poor pooch a bowl of blood every night. I'd rather have the company myself, under almost any conditions. And the dog would outlive him too when you think of it.

All in all, this movie is too good to be dismissed so glibly. It's a good 60's "end of the world" horror flick and I recommend it.

SCENE FROM "NIGHT OF THE LIVING DEAD"? NOPE! IT'S THIS MOVIE.

MONSTER OF PIEDRAS BLANCAS

A nasty looking monster from the sea makes it presence known and upsets various people when it pulls their heads off.

If the *Creature from the Black Lagoon* has a black sheep brother, it's this guy. The monster has a strange looking snarl on his face, and he is certainly more anti-social than his kin, as he prefers ripping people's heads off rather than ogling bathing beauties. The old fashioned fan in me has no problem at all with guys in monster suits. I still find them preferable to the modern CGI "I'm not really there" monster. Even with the cheapest of suits, there's a certain amount of artistry that goes into them. And this is a nice suit, in my opinion, somewhat like the monster in *It, the Terror from Beyond Space*. He looks heavily armored; I don't think it would have an effect to whack him in the head with a crowbar.

Years before I saw the film, I gasped at the picture in Famous Monsters magazine of the creature holding a torn off head. And that wasn't a misleading photo, either. At one point, the monster comes out of a room, holding a severed head by the hair, swinging it back and forth like it's a shopping bag. Later on the beach, we get to see the head again, with a crab crawling on it. (Attack of the Crab Mini-Monster?)

Two other pluses are stars Don Sullivan, *(Giant Gila Monster, Teenage Zombies)*, and Les Tremayne, who appeared in many genre films and had a magnificent voice for radio. You'll also recognize a lot of character actors in a "where have I seen him before?" way. I also appreciate the real lighthouse and location shots.

All things considered, this is a fun film to watch on TV at 1 in the morning.

"DAMN LITTERBUGS!"

NOT OF THIS EARTH

An alien vampire checks out the blood of Earthlings to see if he can keep his race in the red.

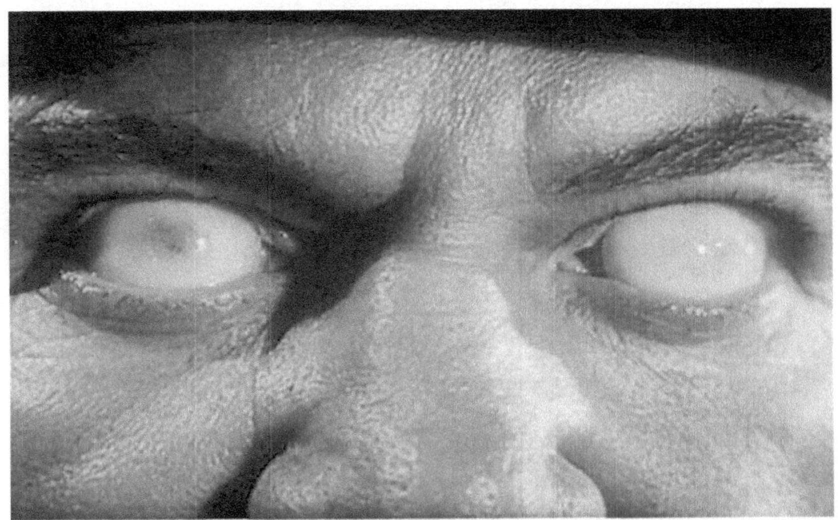

Here's one of the best pre-Poe Roger Corman movies.

The stone faced Paul Birch is perfect as the alien vampire who's scoping out Earthlings for their new fast food franchise. Actually, they want our blood.

They also have an eye problem, or should I say, we have a problem with their eyes. When you look at their all white eyeballs, you die. Here's when looks really do kill.   And what a cast! Besides Birch, we have the beautiful but tough Beverly Garland, the always welcome Jonathan Haze as a sleaze ball, and a great cameo by Dick Miller as a hipster vacuum salesman.

What more could you possibly want?   How about a weird creature that flies around, lands on your head and crushes it? Here is the intersection where cheap effects and actual chills meet. You may laugh at the weird rubber bat like thing flying through the countryside, but when it lands over a guys head and blood pours out from under it, you can't help but go, "Ewwwww!"

So B-movies prove again, that with little money and a fast shooting schedule, you can make an effective, intelligent science fiction movie you don't have to apologize for.

Off and on you can see the back of Paul Birch's stand in, since he apparently walked off the movie after a fight with Corman. I imagine those contact lenses hurt, but it's a very icy look and it's so disturbing when you can't see a person's iris.

Another thing to consider is that both Birch and his replacement at the end are dressed in the black suit, hat and eyeglasses. *Men in Black*? Ahead of its time?

"THAT'S THE LAST TIME I BUY A CHEAP HAIR DRYER OFF EBAY!"

NIGHT OF THE BLOOD BEAST

A man experiences his worst nightmare. He gets pregnant and the father is REALLY ugly.

Can anyone see the movie, *Alien,* in this plot? That movie took from three B's in my estimation.   This one, for the impregnated human, *It, TheTerror From Beyond Space* for its trapped humans with an alien on board, and *Planet of Vampires*, for the giant alien corpse on an abandoned spaceship. Nothing against *Alien*, I like that movie, it's really just an old fashioned monster flick, but these little cheapies can be the inspiration for the big budget extravaganzas.

Like a lot of people my age, you have a fondness for things you saw as a kid in the drive in. This is one of them. The eerie organ theme always scared me, and it was used again in *Beast From the Haunted Cave.*

I still like this film in spite of its uneven production.

I always enjoy seeing Ed Nelson when he shows up in a movie or on an old TV show. He's a Corman regular during this period, and he appeared in a number of classics like *Bucket of Blood.* He made his mark in television on the show, *Peyton Place.* Michael Emmet is also interesting as the pregnant man. He was seen as the illicit lover to Yvette Vickers in *Attack of the Giant Leeches.*

This is one of those movies that's a little confusing as to whom you can believe. The monster claims to be benevolent, but he also wants to take over the earth by melding his people with it. The Earth guys respond like all of them do in these movies; kill the monster, period. No one gets anywhere that way.

"WHAT DO YOU MEAN, I'M PREGNANT?"

The monster is an odd thing with a huge bird like head and looks like he was covered with mud and seaweed. Maybe on his planet he's a snappy dresser but on this one he's kind of icky.

Just don't think too much and enjoy. It's a monster movie. It's short, and it has some interesting features to it.

Let's look at it this way. If some people want to see everything as bad, you can see the good in that same thing and be a better person for it. Now turn to page 45 in your hymnals…

Did that wax statue just move?

There's nothing like a Santo movie. Santo is the real name of this Mexican wrestling hero, and he made a long series of movies in which he fights all kinds of weird creatures, villains, aliens, you name it. In Mexico, they take our pro wrestling tactics even further, by making them superheroes of a sort. When K. Gordon Murray imported these Mex flix into the states, he did us a service but the original film makers a disservice. It's great that we got to see these movies at all, but the atrocious dubbing and awkward translations make what is already a ridiculous movie even more so. But it's also part of the fun. The original movies are meant to be pure mindless entertainment in the first place, so the dubbing, while unfair to the actors, is kind of a plus.The odd thing about this one, other than the fact that Santo never takes his mask off, runs around shirtless 24/7, and always takes time off from crime fighting to throw around some sweaty guy in the ring, is that the villains' motivation is shaky. His face is perfectly all right, but he wants to disfigure everyone else. His hands were turned into shredded wheat in a war camp, but he still manages to make wax figures. The police cite an old photo of the guy and state he doesn't look like he's aged, which makes you expect a *House of Wax* moment where someone pounds off his fake face, but that doesn't happen. Maybe someone forgot, I don't know.

Santo has no problem killing off his enemies, as he "wax" the goons, (get it? "wax"? Forget it.) He pours boiling hot wax on the bad guys and thinks nothing of it.

Santo faces many more monsters over the years including vampires, aliens, mummies, you name it. Sometimes he would

"I WANT TO BE THE MEXICAN VINCENT PRICE'.

team up with another wrestler called the "Blue Demon", so you got a double dose of muscle.

I personally prefer the non wrestling Mexican movies, but when you want to watch something "unique," watch one of these.

MAN WHO CHANGED HIS MIND

Boris plays a shell game with brains.

There haven't been many Karloff movies I could show, but this one fell through the cracks of public domain and is a dandy indeed. Boris is messing around in mad scientist mode again, and while this flick does have some resemblance to the Columbia series of mad doctor movies, it has a unique take on things.

Karloff is supported by the beautiful Anna Lee and a wonderful acid performance by Donald Calthrop as a nasty minded cripple. Anna Lee also starred with Karloff in Val Lewtons' movie, *Bedlam.* She was later a regular on the TV soap, *General Hospital.* A dual performance by Frank Cellier as one who goes from pompous windbag to twisted brain when he's on the receiving end of Calthrops' mind is also a treat.

Karloff, of course, is an enthusiastic nutcase, who gets nastier as the show goes along. John Loder, in what would usually be a dull good guy part, gets into the act when he goes to a brain swap meet. Loder effectively assumes a different persona for the finale.

A well done British chiller, seldom seen, and not to be missed if it comes your way.

THE GIANT GILA MONSTER

A oversized lizard doesn't get along with the locals.

This little oddity was made by the same company that gave us *The Killer Shrews*, which means "Festus" had something to do with it, but overall, it's not as effective as the little critters.

Don Sullivan having fought off *Teenage Zombies* and the *Monster from Piedras Blancas*, ruins a perfectly good hot rod when he uses it as a four wheeled bomb to splatter the hapless lizard. It's hard to tell whether the monster in question is actually evil minded or just a bull in a china shop, but he stomps pretty good either way.

The home made atmosphere of this film and Shrews actually play in its favor. When I watch a low budget film I think, "Okay, it's a low budget film. I'm cool with that," rather then, "Oh God, it's a low budget film, it's automatically a piece of crap!"

Obviously they couldn't afford special optical effects, so the monster and the actors are never seen in the same shot. However, there's some effective low angles of the beastie. When it crawls through the parking lot at the dance, the darkness helps conceal the miniatures. The big guy has a cool theme song as well. Speaking of songs, the film touted some rock and roll "hits" by Don Sullivan.

We hear a few seconds of "My Baby, She Rocks", accompanied by a ball peen hammer in a garage. At the barn party we hear a piece of "I'm Not Made That Way", which sounds like a pseudo Elvis song. But the big offender is the silly, "Mushroom Song," which more people know as "The Lord Said Laugh, Children, Laugh." It's as far from rock and roll as you can get. Unless you consider a ukulele a heavy metal instument.

Don Sullivan is always a likable sort, and he has a French girl friend in this, because I guess, they got a French girl to play the part. Sullivan is supposed to be an up and coming rock singer, but there's very little rocking about his tunes. Fred Graham, an old serial baddie, plays a nice guy sheriff.

There's some cool old hot rods to see in this one if you're into that stuff.

**"CAN YOU MAKE ME SOME HANDCUFFS BIG
ENOUGH FOR A GIANT GILA MONSTER?"**

I saw this in the theater and when you're a kid, you're excited to see ANY monster movie. As an adult, it's not as good, but it's still fun in a nostalgic way.

BLACK SUNDAY

Barbara Steele proves she's still a knock out even with huge holes in her face.

Boy, do I remember the first time I saw this on TV, way back when the UHF channels were these obscure, low power stations that you could pick up by a loop antenna. Usually snowy pictures greeted you, but you could see movies and old TV shows that you

wouldn't see on the regular channels. I first saw the wonderful Rathbone/Bruce Sherlock Holmes movie series on "Sherlock Holmes Theater" on UHF. I saw *Black Sunday* on channel 56 out of Cambridge, MA. Even though parts of it were cut, I was still rather astonished to see what got through. From the time they lifted off the spiked mask from Barbara's face and you saw what looked like boiling egg white surfacing

in her empty sockets, I knew I was seeing something quite unique. Other weird stuff ensued. A coach rolling in slow motion. Her resurrected servant rising from the grave and pulling his mask off, the cobwebs sticking to his face. The old man's head burning in the fireplace. The stake through the eye? The eye? Yeah, the eye! I've never heard of that way to kill a vampire before or since.

Even with a severe case of hole in the face, Barbara Steele is bewitchingly beautiful. She could alternately convey vulnerability and evil with equal fervor. This is one in a long line of Italian horrors she would appear in, but this film is definitely the best one.

Mario Bava shot this in black and white, and I still think it's his best work. Later works in color just don't have the other world eeriness that you can get in black and white. A classic horror film, but don't watch it before going to bed.

ONE OF THE MANY CREEPY PEOPLE IN BLACK SUNDAY! AND THIS IS JUST THE GARDENER!

LITTLE SHOP OF HORRORS

Two and half day wonder from Roger Corman.

Forget the musical. Here's the real deal. A three day wonder knocked off by Roger Corman and written by the underrated screenwriter, Charles Griffith.

Jonathan Haze gets his only starring role in this very black and hilarious comedy. Mel Welles almost steals the show as the language mangling Mr. Mushnick.

There's almost a vaudevillian aspect to the production, as all the characters are broadly painted and act accordingly. There's no one that walks onto this set that isn't memorable, from Dick Miller as the plant eating Fouch, to Jackie Joseph's sweetly naive Audrey, to Charles Griffith's cameo as a crook, to the most famous cameo of Jack Nicholson, who channels Peter Lorre as a pain loving dental patient.

Even the plant, Audrey Jr.s demand, "FEEEEED MEEEE!" has become as symbolic as the The Fly's "HELP MEEE!".

Then throw in a Dragnet parody and you have one delirious movie. The Broadway musical blew it by killing off Mushnick and

"

Audrey, which seemed cruel to me. I didn't even want to see Seymour get eaten, really. He was just a well meaning schlub, who accidentally killed people.

This movie encompasses all the best things about a B movie. It's short, simply and quickly made, but made with an overriding intelligence and sense of fun.

It was a great injustice when the musical was originally produced because they didn't give enough credit to the original screenwriter, Charles Griffith. Without him, they wouldn't have had the cash cow that it became. Griffith was one of Roger Corman's best screenwriters and it's a shame he isn't more well known and respected. I guess B movie writers are second class citizens.

"AWW, SEYMOUR! SHE HAS YOUR EYES!"

BLOOD OF THE MAN DEVIL

Two male witches struggle for control of their coven without actually confronting each other. Something like that.

Boy, is this confusing. Its original title was *House of the Black Death*, which probably makes more sense than the title it ended up with. Apparently this movie was started by Reginald LeBorg, then handed over to Jerry Warren to finish. Imagine being desperate enough to hand a movie over to Jerry Warren voluntarily!

What we end up with is a lot of disparate elements. We have two male witches, one good, one bad, fighting for control of the coven, and another guy with a werewolf curse. There are also scenes, presumably added by Warren, of Katherine Victor hanging out in the forest with some black hooded types, while a bikini clad honey dances endlessly.

On the plus side, this movie has familiar faces, most notably John Carradine and Lon Chaney, but also Andrea King from *Beast with Five Fingers* and Tom Drake from multiple movies and TV shows, best known to genre fans as appearing *The Cyclops*, also with Chaney. Drake is the werewolf, and when he is locked in a room and "turns," we get a quick glimpse of the supposed werewolf's face which as far as I can see is a gorilla mask. At least Lon wasn't subjected to this insult.The biggest crime is we have Carradine and Chaney in the same movie and they share no scenes together. Carradine has long rambling dialog, but Chaney is more fun, with his devil's horns and his gleeful watching of a coven girl gyrating around intermittently. And endlessly. (She must have the same dance teacher as the previous dancer.)

It is darkly shot which helps, and the actors really aren't bad, it's just hard to follow what story there is.

Still, I can't help but like movies like this. There is something about a cheap film being made and getting released that makes me admire the effort.

"I HAVEN'T HAD THIS MUCH FUN SINCE I BROKE UP "THE SONG OF THE NEW WINE" IN FRANKENSTEIN MEETS THE WOLF MAN."

CALTIKI, THE IMMORTAL MONSTER

Globs just want to have fun.

Mario Bava supposedly took over the direction of this film, but whoever did it, delivered some really icky stuff. The monster in question, Caltiki, is a large glob of protoplasm that engulfs whoever is unlucky enough to get in the way. Like its cousin, *The Blob*, the more it eats, the bigger it gets. Some nice chilling effects that got to me when I was young was the diver who got munched on. His uncovered face reveals a jelly covered skull with the eyeballs still intact. More intense still is when the crazed villain gets eaten by Caltiki. We see his head submerged in the goo and his skin withers and falls away until only a skull is left. In a lot of ways, this villain, played by Gérard Herter, is more of a monster than Caltiki.

Caltiki itself was made of a mixture of animals entrails and god knows what else. It doesn't have the nice shiny quality of *The*

Blob; this guy looks more like a malevolent brownie mix. In any case, he's a house buster, as he grows large enough to burst walls.

An Italian movie, it is subjected to the usual awkward dubbing, but the dark moodiness of the entire film makes you forget all that.

All in all, it joins the trio of fun blob movies along with *The Blob* and *X, the Unknown*.

MAN BEAST

A woman goes on an expedition to look for her lost brother in the Himalaya but finds a hybrid human/yeti that wants to start a family.

Jerry Warren is infamous among Z grade movie makers, and for good reason. Most of the time he would take a pre-existing movie, usually a Mexican horror flick, cut it up, even mix it up with another movie, then add boring American scenes of two guys sitting around talking. This one he did almost from scratch, with the use of stock footage, and for Jerry Warren, this is the best of his output in my opinion.

The Beast itself is a pretty cool costume; a white Yeti with a long coat. I assume there was only one suit, so he did multiple shots of the same suit to give the impression of an army of white, hairy guys.

The hybrid yeti guy is kind of creepy with his whitish hair and eyebrows. He just doesn't look or act right. He wants to propagate his species, which in itself isn't bad, it's just that it's far nicer to ask for volunteers rather than take them by force.

For some goofy reason, the "star" of this movie is someone named Rock Madison, but no such person seems to be in the movie. It's a great Hollywood sounding name, but you really kind of need an actual person to go with it. I guess Jerry saved some money that way because it's free to hire a "name" rather than an actual actor. Here's some other names he could have used: Slate Corrigan, Dick Steele, Barry Biceps, Dwayne Torso and Randy Beating.

WANTED: ONE WOMAN WHO LIKES HYBRID HUMAN/YETIS. OBJECT: PROCREATION. LIKES TO HAVE DINNER BY CANDLELIGHT IN DARK CAVES.

When watching Jerry Warren's movies, which should be an Olympic event, you get the feeling that he turns the camera on, goes home, and then comes back and turns the camera off. He likes long master shots and it takes you by surprise when he has a close up. That's why Man Beast seems like the best of his output. It has some variation in shots.

The movie is short and pretty decent for Jerry, but it still is the runner up for worst Abominable Snowman movie, next to *Snow Creature*.

THE MANSTER

Two heads are badder than one.

Just as there are living head movies, there were a few of the "two headed" variety. I think this may be the first one, although head number two doesn't emerge until halfway through the movie. *The Manster* is another one of those movies that people will put down, but I've always liked this movie, and it has truly memorable sequences. If you remember anything about this movie, this Japanese/American hybrid has one of the most unnerving scenes you'll ever see. After the main character starts his personality change, his shoulder irritates him, until he finally pulls back his shirt and what does he see? Or should I say, what sees him? An eye growing on his shoulder. This seems right out of a Salvador Dali film. Truly nightmarish.

I thought the lead, Peter Dyneley was actually an American, but he's a British actor and I think he pulled off the accent quite well. The mad doctor, played by Tetsu Nakamura, appeared in Toho productions and is a familiar face in giant monster movies. His mutated wife is a thing to behold, and I found it actually quite touching when he is forced to shoot her and put her out of her misery. It's also nice that we get to hear the actor's own speaking voice instead of a clumsy dubbed one.

In spite of the cheap looking second head, this movie is effective in the night scenes. Most of the time, they wisely show the two heads in semi-darkness.

The famous "split" at the end, is both outlandish and harrowing at the same time. And having the hairy half of the Manster die in a volcano is a unique way to go. I just wonder now if the human half of the Manster is liable for the murders. He could always plead insanity due to a split personality. And body.

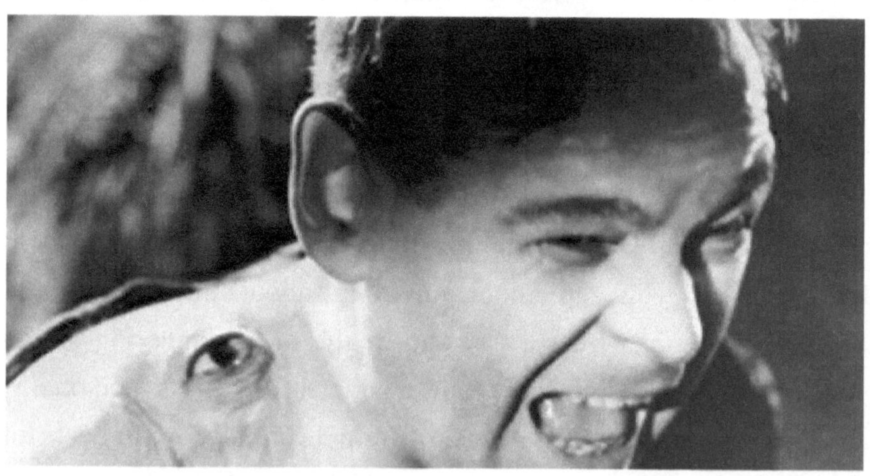

I'VE HEARD OF HAVING A CHIP ON YOUR SHOULDER BUT...

Subsequent two headed movies, such as the *Amazing Two Headed Transplant* and the really ridiculous *Thing with Two Heads*, can't hold a candle to *The Manster*.

KILLERS FROM SPACE

Invaders from outer space have a bad case of ping pong ball eyes.

To me, there is a Holy Trinity of 50's monster movie heroes. They are John Agar, Richard Denning and Peter Graves.

Graves, who is the star of this opus, was also in *Beginning of the End, It Conquered the World,* and the whacked out anti-Commie movie, *Red Planet Mars.* He may be better known to most people as the star of *Mission Impossible* or for his comic turn in *Airplane,* but to me, he is a monster hero. No matter how loony the movie may be, Graves had a solid, believable persona in each role he undertook.

A lot of 50's sci-fiers produced iconic images; the Saucermen, the She Creature, Godzilla, etc, but I think the pop eyed aliens in this one qualify. They look like characters out of an old Tales to Astonish comic magazine. You may laugh at their appearance, but if I ran into a guy with a full length hoodie with his eyeballs protruding halfway out of his skull, I wouldn't laugh at him, I'd run like hell.

The movie is padded, like many of their time, as Graves walks through the cave he's captive in and witnesses back projection of fake dinosaurs and the like.   However, seeing how this movie is made in 1954, I may be wrong, but I think this is the first alien abduction movie. Only about a decade later did alleged real alien abductions become public with the revelations of Betty and Barney Hill in the book *The Interrupted Journey*. W. Lee Wilder, not exactly an ace director, can be credited for this first, and the first Yeti movie, his similarly cheapo, *Snow Creature*.You can sit there trashing this movie in your oh so clever way, or you can just relax and be part of the cheesy fun. It's up to you.

ATTACK OF THE REAR PROJECTION!

KING OF THE ZOMBIES

Some adventurers stumble upon a Nazi stronghold in the jungle which is populated by zombies!

Originally, Bela Lugosi was slated to appear as the bad guy in this one, but instead he was shunted over to *The Invisible Ghost*, which is a shame, because it would have been so much fun to see Bela interacting with the great black comedian, Mantan Moreland. Nothing against Henry Victor, who does a fine job, but what a treat it would have been to see Lugosi and Moreland in the same movie.

This is a favorite among Monogram movie devotees as it's almost as much a comedy as a zombie film. Robert Lowry and Dick Purcell are the "heroes" but the person who saves this film is Moreland. Moreland and other black actors of his time, had to make a living, and usually ended up playing subservient roles. But Moreland took what was the stereotype of the time and through his considerable comedic skill, made it somehow more edgy and contrary to how he was "supposed" to act. His banter with both his white companions and the black members of the household are the

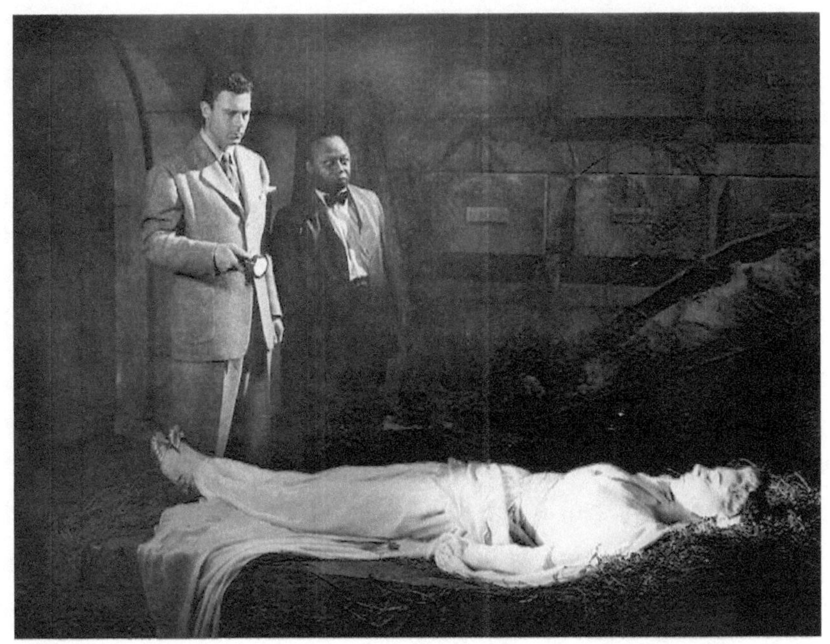

highlights of the movie, and only he seems to have enough sense to be scared of the zombies. These pre-Romero zombies are the mindless servant types of folklore. They are pretty spooky looking, though. My favorite line in the movie is when Moreland is supposedly hypnotized into being a zombie. He walks over to his fellow dead guys and says, "Move over, boys, I'm one of the gang now." If you look instead at the other zombies, you can detect that they're trying to keep from laughing, and I don't blame them. At the end, Purcell, who is also zombified, takes some bullets in the chest, but still emerges alive and unharmed at the end. That zombie formula is pretty impressive; like a mystical bullet proof jacket.

The plot line is similar to a later film, *Revenge of the Zombies*, in that the Nazis think making zombies is a good idea for their war effort. They don't stand a chance against Moreland, though.

THE HIDEOUS SUN DEMON

Even sunblock won't help.

Apparently after Robert Clarke was in *The Astounding She Monster*, he thought he could do better than that. And, in my opinion, he did. The idea of the sun demon is unique; a twist on the werewolf premise. The costume is pretty cool, too.

The movie shows its low budget roots by using real locations and having that sort of "roomy" sound when dialog is spoken. That's when they can't get the microphone close enough to the actor, so the actor's voices lose some "presence". However, I don't hold that against it. Not that long ago, using "real" locations was the norm, replacing the Hollywood set, which was considered artificial. Now we're back to artificial, with a lot of sets both indoor and outdoor not being "real," just CGI.

Poor B movies can't win. If they build a set, the critics will say the sets are flimsy, if they film on location, they get slammed for not using a set.

I must say that Robert Clarke's character doesn't gain much sympathy. He's kind of whiny and belligerent, although I suppose I would be too if I could grate cheese on my arm. His chomping into a rat at one point doesn't help either. He also gets lucky with a busty blonde, (who helps pad out the movie with a song), but he deserts her the next morning, because his morning afters are a bitch.

The final scenes on the water tower are pretty effective too, and how many times do you see a monster fall from a water tower?

Robert Clarke was in better movies, such as Bedlam, Man from Planet X and The Body Snatcher, but as this is the only movie he ever directed, I don't think you can really fault him too much. He

LOW BUDGET, YES. GREAT MONSTER SUIT, YES!

may have gotten better at it given the chance, and there's a lot worse directors around that kept making movies.

Clarke led a pretty interesting life, and worked with a lot of more famous actors. His book, To B or Not To B, makes for an entertaining read. The people that made these kinds of movies usually didn't take them seriously, which is a big plus when the likelihood is that critics will dump all over your movie.

DEAD MEN WALK

Two doses of George Zucco and Frye on the side make a delicious vampire film.

This movie is better than its rep, and is worth the time to watch it at least once. If you had a contest between Lionel Atwill and George Zucco as to who could convey the most evil, I think it would be a draw. Atwill had an almost jovial kind of malice, while Zucco exuded venom through his 100 watt eyeballs. Zucco's voice had a reptilian cadence to it, while Atwill seemed like he could hum a children's tune while he butchered you. Very different types, but both masters at villainy.

Good old George gets to play two parts in this PRC cheapie take on vampires. Again here is another poverty row movie that I feel gets slammed too hard. Critics come down on the cheapness of the whole deal in terms of effects, sets, etc. C'mon! This is poverty row. That's the whole point. To skewer a movie simply because there's no money behind it is like criticizing a rear wheel drive car for not handling snowy roads as well as four wheel drive. Yeah, no kidding, Sherlock! Okay, the scripts weren't that good, and the actors in support weren't top notch, but they are still enjoyable for what they are.

Zucco makes a good differentiation between the good George and the bad George, not just because the good one wears a hair piece, but through their manner and line delivery. PRC even manages some good split screen effects to show the twin Zuccos.

A common phrase among the monster generation is "poor Bela," because he was so misused and mistreated by the big studios. (Although, truth to tell, in many ways, Bela was his own worst enemy.) I say it should be "poor Dwight." Frye was a talented character actor who couldn't find much work after being typed for horror roles. He showed comic ability both as Renfield and Fritz but never seemed to land an out and out comedy role in a non monster movie. Here, we are sadly seeing him in his final days, playing a combination of Renfield and Fritz, but he still puts his all into it. He deserved better than this.

ATTACK OF THE GIANT LEECHES

Giant leeches have a grand old time in the South drinking them lil' ole blood juleps from the locals.

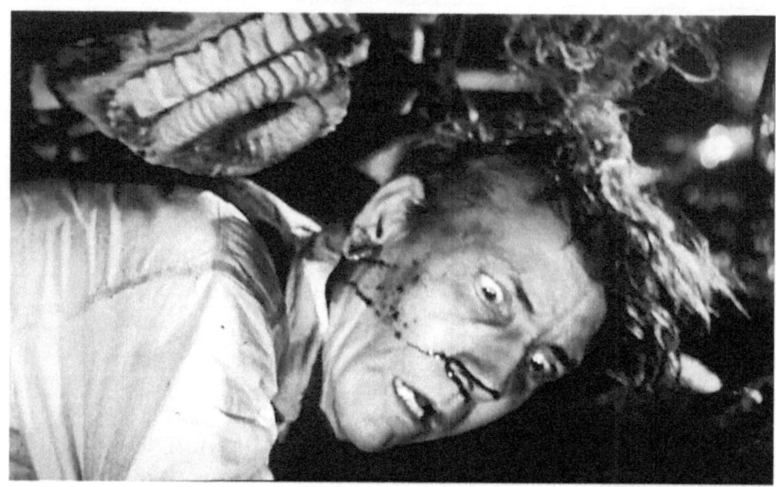

Put together a steamy swamp and steamy Yvette Vickers and we have one humid movie.

Naturally this movie gets lambasted by the smug hipsters who fancy themselves film critics, but for a movie shot for what looks like pocket change, it does have its moments.

First of all, it has a fun cast. Yvette Vickers really doesn't have to do anything but stand there to get the appreciation of the male viewers, but Vickers was a much better actress than most B movie starlets, and I think it's unfair that she didn't move into more substantial roles in so called A budget pictures. She manages to make her character both pathetic and scheming at different intervals. Bruno VeSoto gives the performance of his life here as the wronged husband, eliciting some real pity from the audience. He's not a mean, abusive husband; he just chose the wrong woman to marry. Even she doesn't really hate him, she has some gratitude to him. She married him to get someplace in life, but all it gets her is a date with a big leech.

It's fun to see character actor Gene Roth in these movies. He was a brutal Nazi in She Demons, but here he's a dim bulb sheriff. Roth appeared in many of the Three Stooges shorts, where he is easily recognizable.

Oh, and the poor sap who Vickers is cheating with is none other than Michael Emmet, who also came to a bad end in *Night of the Blood Beast.*

"HONEY, IT'S TIME WE TALKED ABOUT YOUR ACNE PROBLEM."

The leeches seem to be plastic trash bags with suckers stuck on them, (and in them, too). I believe Corman regular Ed Nelson helped make the leech suits, but I don't know if he had to double as a leech. For such a cheap production, there are still chilling moments in this. It uses the same weird theme music that was used in *Night of the Blood Beast*. There's something about those organ chords than goes up my back. The stand out scene is in the underground cave, where the victims of the leeches are lying on the rocks, half alive, so the leeches can feed on them cafeteria style whenever the mood strikes them. The leeches attaching themselves to the victims throats with the blood oozing out is pretty skin crawly. When I was little it also creeped me out when the explosives went off underwater and we see the bodies underwater as they float slowly to the surface.

These kind of movies are just like reading a comic book to me. You watch it on a lazy afternoon or late at night, take it at face value, and never seriously. As for me, I can never get enough comic books or B-movies.

GIANT FROM THE UNKNOWN

A rather large Spanish conquistador rises from the grave and tries to kill the people that woke him up.

Richard Cunha turned out some of the most fondly remembered schlock films of the 50's. This is probably his best feature, although nowhere near as fun as Frankenstein's Daughter. Plus size Buddy Baer is the title monster, and he is indeed an imposing figure in Jack Pierce's makeup. His Spanish conquistador outfit gives him an unworldly look, but it's his silence that makes him frightening. Unfortunately he is a sleeping giant through the first half of the movie, while we wade through some misleading plot points and talky scenes. Good old Morris Ankrum, the go-to guy for generals, doctors and official types, is looking for the Diablo Giant, a legendary nasty Spaniard named Vargas, who may be buried in the hills of this out of the way town. Ed Kemmer, (star of *Space Patrol* and *Earth vs the Spider*), is the hero/love interest for poor Sally Fraser, who is relegated to the typically helpless, useless female role, a customary slot for female actors of the period. She is relentlessly smiling and happy through most of it, doing her womanly duty making coffee and cleaning up for the men who are out doing the "real" work. It makes you wish she'd team up with Vargas. Of course, when she has the chance to run away from Vargas when he comes after her, she faints instead, even though it would have been fairly easy to outdistance the giant, who is out of shape after being buried for a few hundred years. A nice unplanned touch at the end of the film is some unexpected snowfall, which makes the scenes at the cabin and bridge rather pretty to look at it. Vargas ends up doing a swan dive into the dam, so at least he gets all that dirt washed off him. The fun of these movies is seeing the familiar faces. Bob Steele plays the annoying sheriff who wants to arrest Ed Kemmer every five minutes. Steele was a cowboy hero in his heyday, but did some effective dramatic

"NO WONDER THE RENT IS SO CHEAP FOR THIS APARTMENT."

roles in *Of Mice and Men* and *The Big Sleep*. He is also beloved by *F Troop* fans for playing Trooper Duffy. "There we were at the Alamo, shoulder to shoulder, backs to the wall…" One of the unexplained points of the movie is that it starts with the townsfolk complaining about the mutilated cattle and a guy who also got himself killed. This happens before Vargas even gets out of bed, so I wonder who the heck was doing that stuff. Maybe the sheriff was doing it, which is why he's blaming anyone else for it. Hmmm…

THE DEVIL'S PARTNER

***An old man makes a pact with the devil and comes back as an
evil young man who looks just like Ed Nelson.***

Here is one of the things I love about these B-movies; seeing
all these different character actors in one place. I can't really
categorize Ed Nelson as a character actor here, but it is a change of
pace for him, playing a guy who's rotten to the core. We then have
Edgar Buchanan, the gravelly voiced rotund actor who could be a
lovable rogue or an authority figure. Byron Foulger could never be
a lovable anything; he spent his career as a thin voiced, nervous
little milksop type, but he sure does excel at that type of character.
We also have the alligator man himself, Richard Crane, (*Alligator
People*),as another victim of the devil man. The movie is kind of
vague plot wise to say the least. You don't really know what
Nelson's agenda is, other than making people miserable. He can
even turn into an animal when he wants to and uses that power to

turn into a horse, or to control an evil Lassie that scars up poor Richard Crane.

I guess demons don't really need excuses to do what they do, but Nelson gets his payback at the end, and even cashes out looking like his old self, and I do mean old.

Enjoy the actors and don't think too much about the plot and you'll have a devil of time watching this.

***Lot of Italian vampires lurking around during the 1960s. I
guess they liked the food.***

A scientist who discovers a way to revive dead tissue finds out
a little too late that he needs to keep killing women to get more of
the glandular stuff he needs. So he injects himself with a serum
that turns him into a monster so he can kill people without drawing
attention to himself. Makes perfect sense to me.

I tell ya… what we men go through to restore a women's good
looks… couldn't you just stay beautiful so we don't have to get off
the couch and do something about it? I don't think I've ever seen a
movie with a woman scientist going through all this trouble for a
man. I mean, really!   I
first saw this movie at the good old drive in. When I was young, I

wouldn't give a dubbed foreign film a fair look, but as I got older and had seen all the American/British stuff, I ventured into the Mexican and Italian offerings and I'm glad I did. They can make fun B-movies just like we can. And this is fun. The monster is really cool looking, especially when he's running around at night with a hood on. Kind of like the moon killer in the early color horror film, *Dr. X.* Considering we have an odd movie to begin with, there are several extra oddities in this one which I still don't know the answer to. During the course of the movie, the main character's hair goes from dark to almost white for no apparent reason. Maybe he works too hard, I don't know. Also, the first time he transforms into the monster, there is a brief shot of him as a stop motion model! If it isn't stop motion, it sure looks like it. Why they would do this is beyond me. It's an incongruous shot,

"LOOKS LIKE YOU'RE DOWN A QUART."

but I kind of like it. The other thing that is humorous to me nowadays, is to me the doctor sort of looks like Eugene Levy from SCTV.

This Italian movie has the usual kind of dubbing you see in these imports. I've noticed in Italian movies, the dubbing is usually over emphatic and intense, the assumption being that Italians probably talk that way. Being part Italian myself, it would be fun to speak like that in real life. I could say things like, "Please, my darling, pass the salt! I can't live without it!" Then I turn into a monster and go out and kill the mailman.

In any case, the scientist commits all this carnage for love, which is what many men do in real life anyway. Except we don't have any neat Italian sports cars.

SHE DEMONS

When you're a castaway, the last thing you want is to be stranded on an island with some crazy Nazis and some really ugly women.

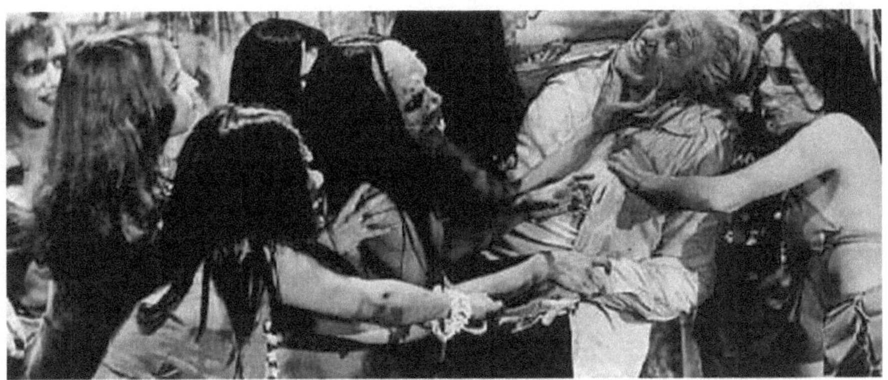

Oh boy! Another how to restore your wife's face movie! Even Nazis get sentimental about how their wives used to look before their looks went to hell in a hand basket.

Another Richard Cunha extravaganza with loony people, monsters and a fun cast of supporting players. Irish McCalla, (who also played Sheena of the Jungle), is a spoiled brat, and the rugged hero is initially at odds with her, but guess what? That's right, they fall in love anyway. Isn't that always the way?

Tod Griffin, the lead guy, isn't really a familiar face to me, but he did mostly TV shows during the 50's and 60's. Here he is the usual generic disposable he-man type. It's the others that offer the fun.

Ms. McCalla of course, is not only nice to goggle at, but she does do a convincing job of annoying us, at least at first. Rudolph Anders was a quick pick to play Nazis, doctors or other authority figures in various films and TV shows. My favorite role of his was as Gottfried in *Frankenstein 1970,* where he was the voice of sanity against Karloff's deranged monster builder. I've seen him in *Adventures of Superman* and plenty of other TV shows. He was also in the cheapie *Phantom from Space*. Another very recognizable face is Victor Sen Yung, most notable as Number 2 son, Jimmy Chan in the famous series. He provides mostly comedy relief in this one, as he did in most of the Chans. Burly Gene Roth, all around character actor and frequent face in B-movies and Three Stooges shorts, plays another nasty Nazi.

Of course the experimental drug that is used to restore faces has only the opposite effect on his guinea pig women; it's makes them, well, She Demons. Funny how these things always go to the extreme opposite of what was intended. What if it turned beautiful girls into more of an average type. That would still be an improvement over what his wife looks like now. But I guess the title *Plain Janes* isn't as dynamic as *She Demons*.

"WHAT DO YOU MEAN MY SWASTIKA DOESN'T TURN YOU ON?

Anders character isn't that devoted to his wife anyway. He hits on McCalla with no hesitation. Maybe he thinks his uniform is sexy. Yeah, pal, swastikas are always a babe magnet.

To kill some screen time, the she demons do a lengthy dance for the bored males in the audience.   I will say they are an attractive bunch. Too bad the Nazi nut case keeps cutting down on the cuteness factor.   Another delirious Richard Cunha flick, fun, goofy, monsters, beautiful girls, evil Nazis; I don't know what's left to throw in the mix. Although it would be interesting if the Monster of Piedras Blancas swam ashore here.

VAMPIRE'S GHOST

A vampire in Africa tries to preserve his existence without any luck.

John Abbott is the titular lead in this oddball vampire movie from Republic Studios. A strange choice in most ways, since Abbot usually played academic types or mild mannered professors and the like. However, he did have the necessary eyeball wattage for this movie, and he uses it to good effect. He also delivers some pathos in the role, since it is a curse he struggles with.

What a strange soup this movie is. First off, not only is there a vampire in Africa, but the natives know how to kill one. With a silver spear! Abbott can also walk around in the daylight as long as he wears sun glasses and a pith helmet. It's hard to imagine Lugosi or Lee walking around like that, but Abbott pulls it off. Also, he doesn't need to drag a coffin of earth around with him, just a nice little box with his grave dirt in it. One cool thing the movie shows is Abbott's reflection in the mirror at a dinner table. We just see his empty clothes. The only other movie I can think of that did that is *Return of the Vampire*, when the vampire hunters put a mirror in Lugosi's coffin while he slept and we saw his upper collar and tie but no head!

One thing that seems unusual as well but actually has a precedent in literature, is that after being injured by a silver spear, Abbott can rejuvenate himself by lying under a full moon. While that sounds more like a werewolf, I'm pretty sure in the early vampire tale, *The Vampire* by Polidori, Lord Ruthven does the same thing, and I know that in the penny dreadful *Varney the Vampire,* he does it as well in that incredibly long vampire serial story.

Since Republic was mostly a serial producer, it's no surprise to see the great Roy Barcroft in a bit as a disgruntled sailor. Barcroft always made a great heavy, especially as Captain Mephisto in *Manhunt on Mystery Island*, my favorite serial. It's weird to see Abbott best him in a fight though; I guess that super strength of bloodsuckers comes in handy.

One of the vampire's victims, played by Adele Mara, has a short, sexy dance number before she gets knocked off by the fickle Abbot.

Grant Withers plays a priest in this one, a strange sight with the clerical collar and the pith helmet. Another B movie regular, Withers was the first Jungle Jim in the serial of the same name, and was the cop in many of the Karloff series of Mr. Wong films.

The vampire is destroyed by fire in this one, the only time I remember one going out that way. Dracula's corpse was burned in *Dracula's Daughter,* but he was already dead. But we know better, don't we?

"I GUESS WE SHOULDN'T HAVE ASKED FOR A TABLE FOR SEVEN."

THE APE MAN

A scientist fools around with a drug that turns him into a hairy ape man. Then he has to kill people to get their glandular fluid so he can revert back to normal, because it's a drag to shave 7 times a day.

"I'VE ALWAYS WANTED A LITTLE BROTHER."

I think now we can say "poor Bela." I often wondered what he thought when he had to perform in this wacky movie. I just know what he did. He gave it his all. That's what makes the movie watchable; no matter how outlandish the premise is, Lugosi takes it all very seriously. His character isn't sympathetic in this one, he's whiny and selfish, and I still don't know what he's trying to accomplish.

This is one of the infamous Monogram nine, and certainly the screwiest one. At one point, hairy Bela and his pet ape walk down the main street at night and no one is around to notice or care. Maybe where he lives a lot of people have their own pet gorilla so seeing one on a stroll with his master is no big deal. Bela also has to talk to his gorilla in gorilla-ese, and threatens him with growls and thrashing his arms.

The supporting cast includes the resident wise guy reporter played by Wallace Ford. Ford managed to get jobs both in B movies and more prestigious productions, and his breezy, quick mouthed person is certainly needed for this one. Minerva Urecal is Bela's sister, and for all the sympathy and support she shows him, she's gets murdered by him as a reward. Louise Curry is the sweet young thing in this one, and although she doesn't have much to do, she is one of the better B lister actresses in these films.

The movie itself knows how ridiculous it all is, when a mysterious man keeps popping in and out, giving tips to the main players. At the end he reveals himself as the writer of the movie as he winks at the audience saying, "screwy idea, wasn't it?" Indeed.

MONSTER FROM GREEN HELL

I don't know where Green Hell is on the map, but it's not one of my vacation choices.

Jim Davis stars in this jungle movie with cameo appearances by big bugs. Producer Al Zimbalist was renown as one of the cheapest men on the planet, and made extensive use of stock footage in his productions. This one is no exception, as Zimbalist hijacked scenes from the movie, *Stanley and Livingston.* In order to match scenes with the stock footage, Jim Davis had to wear dated clothes and an old fashioned pith helmet.

Davis would probably be best known for his role in *Dallas*, but I remember him in an old TV show called *Rescue 8*, and of course, appearances in various movies and TV shows. We monster lovers also know him from *Jesse James Meets Frankenstein's Daughter* and Al Adamson's amusing *Dracula VS Frankenstein.* Hey, the poor guy had to eat, didn't he?

Those movies are actually more fun than this one, because Green Hell plods along and gets mired in a lot of talk.

The best thing about it is the wasps. There was a large wasp head constructed, supposedly designed by the great Paul Blaisdell, with its claws grabbing victims, and at the end we even get some stop motion wasps attacking. If there were more use of this kind of thing or just seeing the monster head poking out here and there, it would have improved the movie quite a bit.

In original screenings the movie print was tinted red when the volcano goes off to kill off the nasty bugs. This is about the only real excitement in this movie, but it's still better than a Jerry Warren movie.

"I'LL TRADE MY HAT FOR YOURS."

WHITE ZOMBIE

Bela Lugosi in one of his most famous roles as the evil zombie master in this low budget classic.

Bela Lugosi edges out George Zucco for the prize of the most mesmerizing eyes. He puts them to full use in this early talkie.

In case you didn't know, zombies in the original sense, are not flesh eating ghouls, nor do they have designs on eating your brain for a mid afternoon snack. They are the dead brought back to a mindless existence to serve as uncomplaining slaves; in this case, working the sugar cane fields at night.

The word "zombie" first come into public awareness in W. B. Seabrook's book, *Magic Island.* Apparently there was even short lived play called Zombie, inspired from the book.

White Zombie is the first zombie movie. It was made by the Halperin brothers, who although they made movies after this, never duplicated the somber, eerie feel of this movie.

Lugosi has a field day playing Murder Legrande, (what parent would name their child, Murder?) and he is the main reason for the film's success. Keep in mind, this is an early talkie, and a more naturalistic style of acting wasn't yet the de ri·gueur in movies. (Didn't think I knew a word like de ri·gueur, did you?)   I think Robert Frazer comes off second best in the cast, especially in the scene where he is slowly losing his will after digesting Lugosi's instant zombie powder. The zombie expert is meant to be amusing, but I find him rather annoying with his constant asking for a match. He also creates a contradiction in his view of zombies, as he tends to relate their condition as drug induced. Later however, the zombies are shot in the chest and they still walk. That would be some drug if it makes them bullet proof.

The zombies themselves are scary looking as hell, due to makeup genius, Jack Pierce, loaned out from Universal for this production. And the actors playing the zombies have just the right glassy eyed stare, which Tor Johnson would later turn into a career.

The movie has plenty going for it. Although there is sporadic music, there's more silence overall, and the most effective scene is when the zombies work the mill, turning the wheel which leads to a pit housing the blades that cuts the sugar cane. On the catwalk above, a zombie loses his footing and falls into the blades, and not a sound is made, no screams of pain, just the monotonous grind of the wheel. It's chilling and understated.

There are practically no day scenes in the movie, and the use of light in both exterior and interior scenes paint a black atmosphere of dread.

So many wonderful shots: Lugosi's hand taking away Madge Bellamy's scarf as the couch departs, Lugosi's eyes in pin light close ups, a shot from the interior of the crypt as the coffin is rolled in, a clever shot of the shadows of people dancing in a cafe, as Joseph Cawthorn sits alone in despair at a table.

It's a piece of horror film history and deserves its place among the classics of 30's horror.

TERROR IS A MAN

If you hurt the kitty, kitty will scratch you. To death.

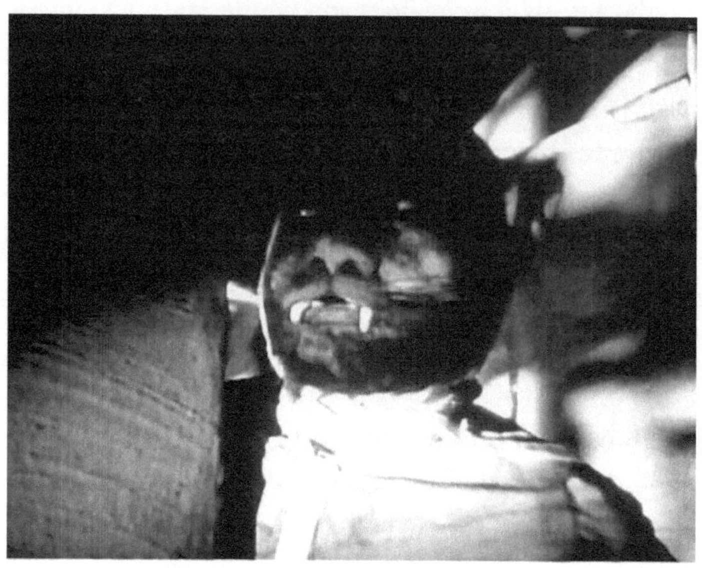

My favorite H.G. Wells book is *The Island of Dr. Moreau*, which is also his most moody and eerie novel. One genuine masterpiece of cinema was made from it, that being *Island of Lost Souls* with Charles Laughton as Dr. Moreau. A pre-code film, it was shocking in its time and was banned or censored in various places. In the late fifties, one of the first, if not the first, horror flicks made in the Philippines which traveled to the states was this one, *Terror is a Man*.

Francis Lederer, who made a fine Dracula in the film, *Return of Dracula*, is the obsessed surgeon here as he experiments on a single animal, a panther. Lederer seems more reasonable than Moreau ever did, but that doesn't keep him torturing the poor animal to prove a point. Richard Kerr is shipwrecked on the island and becomes a reluctant bystander. He's repulsed by the experiments, but he wouldn't be alive it weren't for Lederer. One person who isn't repulsive is Lederer's wife, played by Greta Thyssen. After seeing her in this movie, it's weird to see Greta in one of the Three Stooges shorts with Joe Besser. There seems to be a requirement in many horror films that the middle aged madman is married to a beautiful young woman. The wives never have any trouble falling in love with the first hunk that comes along, so I guess they're not matches made in heaven. For her part, though, she sympathizes with the tortured beast, and it's easy to see why she'd want to get the hell off cut-em-up island.

The panther man is an interesting creature, as he is usually wrapped up in bandages, or shown in semi-darkness. From what you can see of the makeup, it's very well done, and the angry sounds it makes are chilling. He is indeed formidable once he's free of his straps. You can't help feeling sorry for it though, and Lederer gets what he deserves at its hands, er, claws.

"I TOLD YOU BEFORE! DON'T BRING THOSE THINGS INTO THE HOUSE!"

One silly thing is a bell that rings right before a "shocking" scene when a scalpel cuts into the flesh of the creature during an operation. There was a notice at the beginning of the film that the bell would sound before a shocking scene occurred, in case you wanted to turn away. It's hard to tell what's being cut, some real animal flesh or foam rubber, but considering the all out carnage we see today, it's rather quaint. The bell sounds like an alarm clock, and I expect Lederer to stop what he's doing and say, "Oops, got to stop and pick up the kids at school."

That aside, this is really a creepy, well made variation on Dr. Moreau and I recommend it.

REVENGE OF THE ZOMBIES

Yet another Nazi doctor wants to make a zombie army. But the zombies don't always want to cooperate.

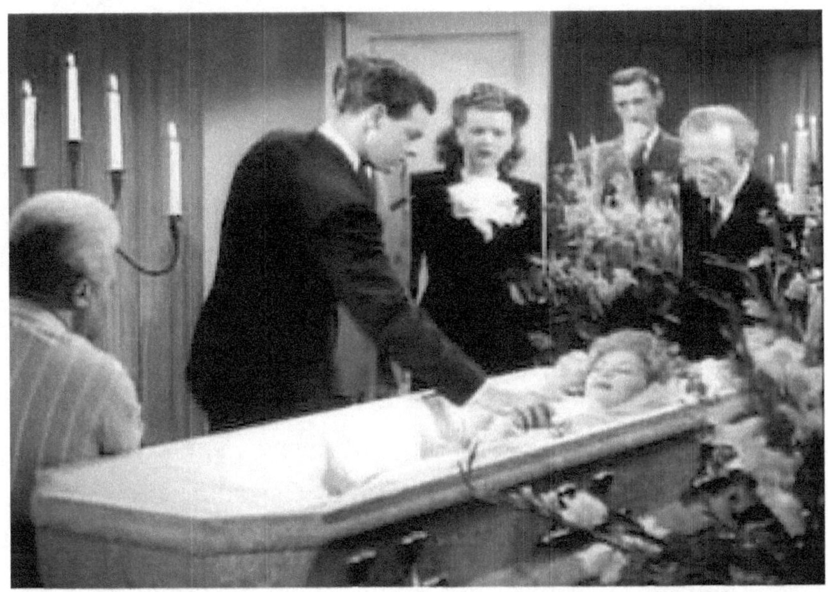

In a sort of follow-up to *King of the Zombies*, this time John Carradine takes the helm as the fanatic Nazi scientist striving to create zombie cannon fodder.

For a Monogram movie, it is much more polished than usual. The films' opening is great and spooky as one of the zombies calls the others to go to work. The wind is howling, the night is full of shadows, and the walking dead rise from their boxes and trudge to their work stations. It's never quite that atmospheric again, but there is still fun to be had.

Mantan Moreland makes a welcome reappearance apparently playing the same "Jeff" from King of the Zombies. Unfortunately he isn't in this one enough. He has some nice comic bits both solo and with the maid which lighten the proceedings. Also on hand is

Bob Steele, former cowboy hero, and hero to monster kids in *Giant from the Unknown* and *F Troop*.

Here he does double duty as a double agent, playing both the hick sheriff and a Nazi compatriot to Carradine.

Carradine gets a big intro that only he could pull off. We see his back first, then he swings around as the camera closes in on his face. His face is mostly hidden by a surgical mask, so we only see those Carradine eyes staring at us. Yet another recognizable face is Robert Lowry as the hero. We know him from *The Mummy's Ghost,* (my favorite Kharis movie), and other epics. He was also the second person to play Batman in a movie serial, *Batman and Robin*.

Veda Ann Borg is the obstinate zombie, the one capable of overcoming Carradine's hypnotic influence. She's the heroine, really, since she's the one that gets rid of Carradine in the end. It's one of those goofy endings where Carradine seems to simply let her lead him into the quicksand to die, when he could have easily broken away from her and ran like hell. At least Karloff had an excuse in *House of Frankenstein*, his back was broken, but Carradine had to pay for his crimes somehow, didn't he?

THE ZOMBIES INSIST ON HAVING WEEKENDS OFF.

THE ASTOUNDING SHE=MONSTER

A glowing babe from outer space throws a monkey wrench into Robert Clark's peaceful day in the mountains.

We can thank this movie for the *Hideous Sun Demon*; and I do thank it. I like the Sun Demon and I like Robert Clarke. Robert Clarke, however, didn't think much of this movie, and that planted the seed in his mind that all non-film makers think: "I can make a better movie than this."

For the first part of the film, you may think this is another movie that is almost totally narrated; fortunately, that stops after about 10 minutes or so. However, the bad news is that almost every shot in the entire film is in a medium long shot. And long takes. I mean, looooong. I've seen cheap movies but this one really takes the cupcake. A handful of actors, one set, practically no special effects and big chunks of film where the camera just sits there and runs, shifts maybe a foot or two left or right, then the camera man turns it on again, takes a nap…you get the idea.

The She Monster of the title is supposed to be a peaceful emissary from another planet, but we don't find that out until the end. Before that, she kills a snake, a dog, a criminal, a bear, (actually a bear rug), a woman and another criminal. She mostly kills in self defense, but not always. In other words, she's a lousy peaceful emissary. Shirley Kilpatrick, who plays the alien, is also busting out all over; so much so that she ripped the back of her costume open when she leaned down. They didn't have time to repair the costume, so except for one shot where you see her back, (pre-ripped, I assume), she is always facing the camera, and when she exits, she walks backwards. She kind of glows in some double exposed way, which gives her some pizzazz anyway, and her arched eyebrows are out of sight. As far as I know, she never appeared in another movie. She would have been an interesting person to interview.

The main criminal is reliable Kenne Duncan, who usually appeared in serials, but is also renown for being in the Ed Wood classic, *Night of the Ghouls*. Most of the film has he and Robert Clark arguing and threatening each other.

The movie isn't long time wise, but it seems long. If only they had more shot variations, things like CLOSE UPS, and cutaways to make it more visually interesting.

What can I say? Probably at the bottom of anyone's list of sci-fi movies, but it got released and Robert Clarke made a better film after this experience. Behind every dark She Monster is a Sun Demon.

WEREWOLF IN A GIRL'S DORMITORY

A werewolf gives out more than failing grades to students in a girls reform school.

The Italian name for this movie is *Lycanthropus*, which is a more dignified title but doesn't have the alluring sleaziness of the American title. The US version also has a brief piece of the song, *Ghoul in School*, by the Fortunes. I finally got to hear the whole song on Youtube. Don't know if it was made for this movie, or just tagged onto it for exploitation sake.

I saw this movie as part of a double or triple feature in a drive in when I was pretty young. Strangely enough, the most terrifying thing to me in this film was the sight of the wide eyed corpse of one of the victims. The face gave me nightmares for a long time. Looking at it now, it appears that the actress was able to do one of those turn your eyelids inside out tricks, or it was some make up device. Anyway you "look" at it, it gave me the heebie jeebies.

This is another movie that gets unfairly denigrated, probably by people giving it a cursory glance. For one thing, I love the look of the werewolf in this. He leans more towards the human side, ala Henry Hull in *Werewolf of London*, and I've always found that very effective. It's also funny to see a werewolf wearing a suit, but this is an Italian werewolf, so maybe he wants to look sharp if he runs into a she wolf. I will admit that it is too talky a lot of the time, but I find most Italian horror films suffer from that. (So do a lot of American ones.)

One of the actors in it, Luciano Pigozzi, always looked like Peter Lorre to me, especially in this one. He's played in other Italian horrors as well.

The lighting is moody and the forest scenes and the sequence where the werewolf is chained up in a basement are well done.

The film is played as a mystery as in "who is the werewolf?", but it's pretty obvious who it is. Curt Lowens, the school master, does garner some sympathy as the hairy one, as does his devoted lover, Leonor, played by Grace Neame.

Yeah, there's the usual bad dubbing, but this is a good B movie which has a lot going for it in my opinion.

"HA HA HA! THAT'S A GOOD ONE! NOW LET ME TELL YOU ONE!"

THE GHOUL

Boris get buried with an Egyptian scarab with which he hopes to attain eternal life. But he dies anyway. Sort of.

I used to see tantalizing pictures from this in *Famous Monsters of Filmland*, when it was considered a lost film. Consequently it was found and restored; however it turned out to be somewhat of a disappointment.

Karloff starts off ugly and dies at the beginning. Then he's gone for a big chunk of the middle. He comes back with a bang, though, for the last third. It's also disappointing that he's not really a reanimated corpse, just the old excuse of catalepsy.

Not that this is a bad movie, it just needed more ghoul. The cast is wonderful. The always enjoyable Ernest Thesiger is one of the greedy crew, and actually has more screen time than Karloff. We have Cedric Hardwick, not bothering with a hair piece for this one, and looking like something out of Dickens. Ralph Richardson appears in an early role before going on to greater fame. I wonder what he would have thought if you told him at the time that he'd wind up as the crypt keeper in the movie, *Tales from the Crypt*?

I wonder why they started out with Karloff already looking ugly as hell at the beginning. It would have been effective if he didn't get monstrous looking until after he escaped from the crypt.

The movie has the usual kind of comedy relief, a man hungry spinster who wastes a lot of screen time trying to land a man. Add to that the young couple initially at odds who get cozy as it goes along help to slow the film down even more.

A rather surprising gory scene at the end occurs as Karloff cuts up his chest in a blood sacrifice.

I'm always to happy to see Karloff and Thesiger in anything, and I'd rather have a disappointing found film than a lost "great" film.

THE STRANGLER

A demented mama's boy takes out his frustration by strangling young women. Not the best of dating strategies.

I have always loved Victor Buono. I don't know when I first saw him, but he proved himself time and time again to be an accomplished dramatic actor and a skilled comedian. His King Tut on the series *Batman* is a tour de force of broad comedy, but he could also play a seriously dangerous person as he does in this movie.

Of course, having a horror like Ellen Corby for a mother is enough to make anyone want to strangle somebody, anybody.

Buono does manage to elicit some sympathy in the role; he is the stand in for every male that gets rejected by women for their looks or weight, except he takes the rejection too far.

Seemingly inspired by the Boston Strangler, the movie has a gritty, almost documentary flavor to it, and is well acted by the

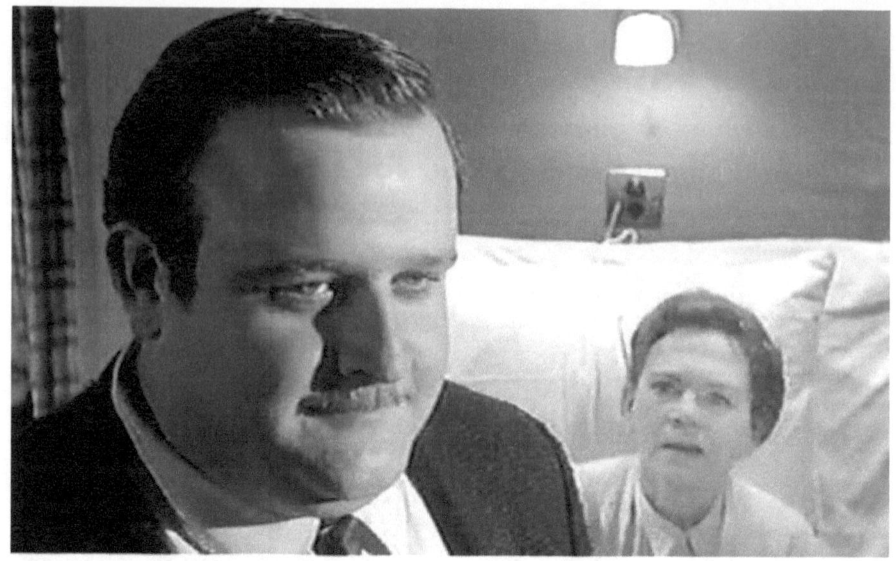

cast. It is a fairly obscure film, I first learned of it in the old magazine, *Horror Monsters* or *Mad Monsters*, can't remember which, but it was many years before I caught it on TV. It was worth the wait, and it's worth your time too.

It's such a shame that Buono died so young. He could have played so many different kinds of roles throughout a long career had he lived. You can still catch him on plenty of old TV shows like *Wild, Wild West, Man from UNCLE, Voyage to the Bottom of the Sea, Perry Mason* and the like. He first came to real prominence in *What Ever Happened to Baby Jane?* and had a smaller role in *Hush, Hush, Sweet Charlotte*. If you want to see him in a really weird movie, catch *Moon child.*

I often wonder how he and Bette Davis got along.

THE WASP WOMAN

A cosmetics queen finds the secret of youth with wasp jelly. She gets stung.

Susan Cabot plays the waspy one in this Roger Corman quickie. She's quite effective as the aging CEO of a cosmetics firm who seeks to restore her beauty by taking a chance on a crackpot experiment. Naturally, since she's using wasp jelly for the formula, she turns into a wasp.   She should have saw that coming. Amusingly, the doctor behind the wasp serum is character actor, Michael Marks, who played Maria's father in *Frankenstein* way back when. I guess he's getting even by turning people into monsters now.

Anthony Eisley and Barboura Morris are the romantic leads. I've always liked both of these actors. Eisley did his share of B and Z movies, most notably Al Adamson's *Dracula vs Frankenstein.* I always thought he looked like a real life version of Tony Stark aka Iron Man, and he could have easily played him had they made an Iron Man movie back then. Barboura Morris enjoys one of the largest roles she ever had as an almost victim of the neck

FOR TELEVISION BROADCASTS EXTRA FOOTAGE WAS ADDED TO FILL TIME.

chomping wasp woman. I find her an appealing actress and wish she could have garnered larger parts in her career. She tragically died way too young at 43 from cancer.

Bruno Ve Soto makes a comic appearance as a night watchman who also meets the sting of death. You can tell he's the comedy relief; the appropriate funny music accompanies him. The score is by Fred Katz, who had a distinctive and quirky style which adorned more than a few B movies.

Susan Cabot is another actress that deserves credit for putting her best into a role. Unfortunately, the make up for the wasp monster is very cheap and is wisely shown in brief spurts. Cabot had another tragic end; murdered by her own son. Some of these people lived in a B movie.

All in all, a very fun movie to watch, plus you never know which version you'll see! When it was sold to TV, the running time wasn't long enough for a time slot, so extra scenes involving Michael Marks were shot to pad out the length. They were tacked onto the original beginning that starts with the office scene. I've seen it both ways since I originally saw this in the drive in.

MAD MONSTER

A mad doctor, (is there any other kind?), creates a wolf man to get even with his enemies. Me, I'd just ring their doorbell and run away.

Oh boy! Two of my favorite people are in this one; George Zucco and Glenn Strange. George really carries a grudge too far in this one, as he injects his poor half witted servant, Pietro, played by Glenn Strange, with a serum that turns him into a…dare I say it?…MAD MONSTER!

This is the only time PRC edged close to a werewolf theme, even though Glenn is a serum induced one. He's got the right look, though, hairy with pointy teeth and claws. You do feel sorry for him though, as he really doesn't know what he's doing, and in his human form, he's just a big, dumb guy.

George, however is another story. He's fit to be tied because his colleagues scoffed at his theories. But no wonder, George can't even make his hallucinations go his way. When he imagines the ghostly images of his enemies surrounding him, they pelt him with all sorts of insults and put downs, and George tries to defend himself. I realize that's what happened in real life and he's reliving it, but if I went through the trouble of hallucinating about it, I'd get even with those guys; pull their ties, pour molasses down their backs, throw ice water down their pants. But then we'd have a short movie that way, so George takes the hard way out and uses Glenn to wipe out his foes, which he manages to do pretty effectively.

A daring scene for its time is when the mad monster kills a child offscreen. You just didn't do that in movies in the 40's most of the time. I was amused by the mother being played by Mae Busch, who was a constant and wonderful foil for Laurel and Hardy. I half expected Stan and Ollie to come knocking at the door looking for work.

The heroine, Anne Nagel, spent most of her acting career in these poverty row gems and in serials. Johnny Downs, the male lead, was actually one of the kids in Our Gang comedies during their silent days.

My thoughts on Glenn Strange. To the monster kids of my generation, Glenn was probably the first time we laid eyes on Frankensteins' monster, due to the frequent TV showings of Abbot and Costello meet Frankenstein. His face became an icon in itself, as even the Don Post studios made a rubber mask in his image. I thought he looked great myself, and his stature certainly helped the role. He had a lot to do in *A&C meet Frankenstein*, but it's still kind of a gyp that he had so little to do in his namesake picture, *House of Frankenstein*. Dracula had more screen time in that one, and it wasn't even his house! The monster got up off the table long enough to throw J. Carroll Naish out a window, and then rather witlessly drag Boris Karloff into the quicksand. His role was even more thankless in *House of Dracula*; I think he was active for about thirty seconds, and they even cut in old shots of Chaney's monster during the fire. They should have given Glenn much more to do in HOF; at least come to life halfway through the movie. In any case, scores of people still love you, Glenn!

As a side note, Glenn plays a monstrous type with similar makeup in the Bowery Boys movie, *Master Minds*. During the movie, Glenn's personality gets switched with Huntz Halls', and you get to see Glenn mimic Hall's physicality as he mouths the dubbed words. It's hilarious!

DAUGHTER OF DR. JEKYLL

The daughter of the infamous doctor claims his inheritance in more ways than one, or does she?

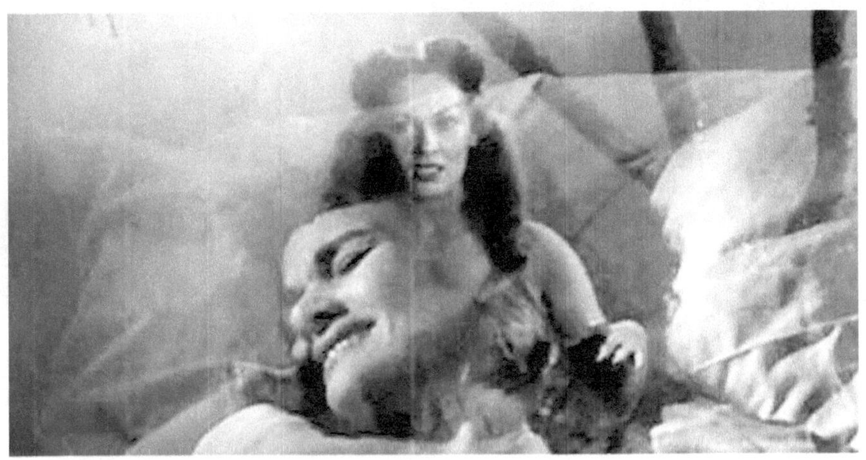

Are you surrrrre?…heh heh heh!

I got such a kick out this movie the first time I saw it. The opening with Mr. Hyde addressing the audience with an echoey "are you surrrre?" just made me chuckle. For some reason it's repeated at the end with a different voice dubbed in. I can't tell for sure if it's actually the actor, Arthur Shields, or a stand in. If it is Shields, they give the whole mystery away at the beginning.

How can you really complain about a movie directed Edgar Ulmer, with both John Agar and Gloria Talbot starring in it? Plus, there's a real monster in this one, not a bogus one like in the lame *Son of Dr. Jekyll*. If you're a sourpuss, go ahead, complain, but not me. I think this movie provides a lot of fun if you're willing to overlook the weird aspects of the story.

Of course, you always can wonder when Dr. Jekyll sired any children, since he was never married, unless Mr. Hyde did some impregnating in his off hours. Also, they can't really seem to figure out what Mr. Hyde is. They call him a werewolf, but they stake him at the end like a vampire. He does transform like a werewolf since he doesn't seem

to take any serum to accomplish that. So, really, what is Hyde in this one?

Making an appearance in this is John Dierkes, the tall, Rondo like character actor who played a menacing henchman to Karloff's Dr. Jekyll in *Abbott and Costello meet Dr. Jekyll and Mr. Hyde.* (So maybe this is the brother of that character, only this time he has it in for Mr. Hyde.)

Ulmer uses the sets and outdoor scenes pretty effectively for a cheap film, and also makes use of the technique of red lens filters to slowly show the lines appear on Arthur Shields face as he transforms for the last time.

Shields was Barry Fitzgerald's brother, and he looks and sounds like him quite a bit. He got a lot of bit roles in his career but this is probably one of his largest roles.

This is another movie that was padded for TV release. During Talbott's drug induced dream sequence, they sandwiched in shots from *Frankenstein 1970.* Hey, why not? It's a dream, it doesn't have to make sense. They also did that annoying double printing of frames at times which gives a jerky motion to the action.

Our man, John Agar, is kind of a bystander for the most part, since Gloria is the center of attention. Agar doesn't even get to kill the monster. Better luck next time, John.

VALLEY OF THE ZOMBIES

A sort of vampire makes things tough on the city morgue.

Republic Studios churned out a lot of B westerns and made some of the best movie serials of all time. However, they did venture into the horror field with a handful of movies that are unique to the genre.

First of all, this is a very misleading title. There are no zombies. There isn't a valley; not even a pot hole. The valley of the zombies is only mentioned in passing, as this story is much more of a vampire outing than anything else. What would zombies be doing in a valley anyway? Going after valley girls?

Ian Keith, with the great character name of Ormand Murks, keeps himself alive with other people's blood, then he embalms the corpses just for fun, I guess. This movie gives you a good look at what Keith might have been like if he had been cast as Dracula in the 1931. He's got the gaunt face, penetrating eyes, and the most reptilian voice on earth. Keith appears mostly in B movies, like this one and *Fog Island* and one or two of the Monogram Chan movies. If you want to see him in a classy picture though, catch him in *Nightmare Alley* with Tyrone Power. He's really very good when he's not chewing the scenery.

Another welcome face is Thomas E. Jackson, who seemed to make a career out of being a tough talking policemen. I remember him first as the cop gunning down Edward G. Robinson in *Little Caesar*, but he was a cop in another Monogram quickie, *Face of Marble*.

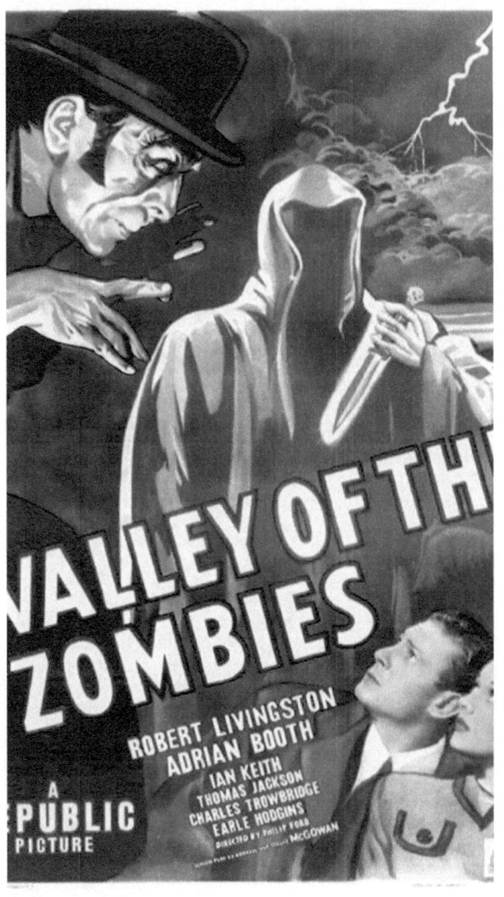

Robert Livingston is the good guy, and is better known for his western roles in serials and the like, while his gal pal Lorna Gray also cavorted in serials at Republic.

There is a lot of humor in this one, intentional, and I think it helps in this case not hinders.

Republic was good with sets, lighting and action scenes and this is no exception.

Other Republic horrors include *Vampire's Ghost, Catman of Paris, The Lady and the Monster, Woman Who Came Back* and one of my favorites, *The Girl Who Dared* which is distinguished not only by Roy

Barcroft's presence, but has Superman alumni Kirk Alyn of the serial, and John Hamilton who played Perry White in the classic TV show.

TEENAGERS FROM OUTER SPACE

A group of aliens land on earth to see if they can use Earth as grazing land for their giant lobster herds. Oh, and instead of grass, the lobsters would eat us.

I really have to admire movies like these. Here is a pretty much unknown film maker making this cheap science fiction feature and getting Warner Brothers to distribute it. Of course, they hung the "teenage" tag on it to attract the drive in crowd, but still, how many producers can say they pulled something like that off?

Better still, it's yet another B movie cult classic, probably because it's considered a "bad" film, but for the more discerning, it's still a fun diversion on a rainy afternoon.

There are two identifiable actors in this. One is Harvey B. Dunn, known mostly for the Ed Wood films, *Bride of the Monster* and *Night of the Ghouls*. Here he is the cute old grandpa looking out for his cute granddaughter who just happens to have a crush on the alien played by David Love. The other familiar actor is King Moody, who went on to play various character parts over the years, but I know him most from *Get Smart* as Siegfried's henchman, Starker.

The guy behind all this is Tom Graeff, who plays the reporter. He apparently wrote, directed, shot and edited the whole shebang, for which I applaud him. I like someone who does everything. Graeff was quite a character by all accounts. After this film, he put an ad in the trades proclaiming himself Jesus Christ II. He did get a job as a film editor for a while, but the poor guy didn't like the cards life had dealt him and he committed suicide in 1970. Too bad. If he had hung a little longer he could have been a fixture at fan conventions.

THEY REALLY USED MIRRORS IN THE BARREL TO MAKE THE GUN FLARE. THAT'S WHAT I LIKE ABOUT CHEAP MOVIES. YOU HAVE TO BE RESOURCEFUL.

Paul Blaisdell, the great monster maker for American International, is uncredited on the production, but I imagine he made the mock up of the spaceship.

The giant lobsters, called the Gargan, show up at the end and are merely a rather shadowy matte plastered on the landscape. It's not well done, but it's better than talking about them and never showing them. The only other major props are two skeletons. One of a dog, (heaven knows where that came from), and one human skeleton, which comes in handy several times, as the aliens like to ray gun their victims into bone town.

The whole movie is dubbed. I understand it was weirdly done. The dialog was pre-recorded, as opposed to the studio procedure of looping it afterwards, and the sound was played on set with the actors mouthing their own words. It works, though, maybe even better than a K. Gordon Murray Mexican dub.

I saw this in the drive in. I believe it was on a double bill with Gigantis, the Fire Monster. (Gigantis was the name Godzilla used when he was moonlighting.)

BEAST FROM HAUNTED CAVE

A bunch of crooks gets their plans upset by a weird monster that camps out in a cave.

Here we have a Gene Corman production, which even without brother Roger's hand behind it, still delivers some good chills and an interesting bunch of characters.

Richard Sinatra, a relative of old snake eyes himself, walks the thin line between good guy and bad guy, and does a decent job at it. You can't really hate the guy, but you wouldn't really trust him either. We also have a crook who falls for a fat Indian woman, which is kind of sweet until they both get knocked off by the wet blanket monster. For the real rotten villain, you have to go to Frank Ward, playing Alexander, who has no redeeming characteristics at all. For the hero role, Michael Forrest checks in, and I recognize him from various roles on TV and the like. I know he was in at least one *Outer Limits* episode. The gangs moll with the heart of gold, Gypsy, played by Sheila Noonan, doesn't succumb to any stereotype here and I like her performance.

Now we come to the monster. When I saw this film as a kid, I didn't think much of him. Having viewed it multiple times now, and having read

how the monster was thrown together with chicken wire and tons of webbing, I can only admire the imagination. Since nothing like it exists in nature, (at least I hope not), you can't say it's inaccurate. If anything, it resembles an arachnid of some sort, since it catches people in webs and sucks the juice out of them to live. There's a shock shot of victim wrapped up in a tree, and there's the scene in the cave where the monster is piercing the neck of his female victim. With the sounds that follow, it reminded me of a similar scene in *Attack of the Giant Leeches*, which was a joint Gene/Roger Corman production.

This flick was directed by Monte Hellman, who went on to more of a career doing unusual films, some with Roger Corman.

All in all, this is a very different kind of B monster film, with more than expected character shadings in it. And it has that same eerie organ theme that *Night of the Blood Beast* and *Attack of the Giant Leeches* had. That music always creeps me out.

BRAIN FROM PLANET AROUS

***It's the battle of the brains as two aliens fight over John Agar.
You gotta love it.***

I just love this movie. I think it's the most fun science fiction
B movie to ever come out of the 50's. How can you resist John
Agar and two floating brains?

Agar, who I always thought was underrated as an actor, has the
time of his life in this one, getting to alternate between a good guy
and a very evil possessed guy. I don't know if he ever really played
an out and out villain before, but he's one of those smiling villains
that's creepy as all get out. You can tell he likes blowing up planes
in flight; gets a good laugh out of it. Those silver eyes of his really
scared me when I first saw it as a kid in the 60's. There was always
something about weird eyes that frightened me as a child; maybe
because it's the slightness of the difference that's unnerving, as if

someone's nose was under their left eye instead of centered.

The music track helps make this movie as well. The thump-thump-thump of the chords when Agar is possessed just magnifies the eeriness of his eyes.

The brains are endearing; sure they seem to be balloons or whatever suspended by wires, but the

movie wouldn't have been the same if they were realistic. I would love to see an Arous brain balloon at the Macy's Thanksgiving Day parades. There should be a special monster parade on Halloween with balloons of the Creature from the Black Lagoon, Kronos, Gort, the She Creature, Beulah from It Conquered the World, etc. Would someone get going on making that happen, please?

This is one of those movies that looks like it was lifted from one of the old science fiction comics in the 50's, and it's that comic book flavor that makes you accept everything that happens.

There are effective shots int his one. The best one being the scene when we see Agar's face behind a water cooler, the distortion of the water combined with his silver eyes makes for a disconcerting shot. Also when Agar looks through the window blinds and blows up a plane is chillingly done.

The most inane thing is at the end when Agar is told by his fiancé that the dog was possessed by another alien brain. He scoffs at her with the line, "what an imagination!" Did he miss what he just went through? A little open mindedness here, John, please.

Robert Fuller has a brief role at the beginning before he boarded the TV show *Wagon Train*. And the ever reliable Thomas B. Henry in on hand. Whenever I watch an Allied Artists or American International movie I wait for Thomas B. Henry to show up. Either him or Morris Ankrum. You can't have a 50's science fiction B movie without one of those guys.

HALF HUMAN

A rare man beast is discovered in the mountains of Japan and human beings waste no time in killing it.

Ah, John Carradine…how he loved to work. When asked by a fellow actor why he would appear in bad movies he replied, "The color of the money is the same." You can't fault him; he had to make a living. Actually, he's done worse than this, and it's a shame that the least interesting parts of this movie were the newly shot American framing story. The movie it encapsulates, a Toho production directed by Ishiro Honda himself, looks like it would be an interesting movie on its own.

At first glance it might seem like a Jerry Warren crazy quilt, but it isn't, it's better. The bulk of the movie is the original Japanese film. The added scenes shot in the USA are there for exposition and padding since the original film is cut to shreds. Unlike a Jerry Warren movie, however, the camera actually moves sometimes, and there is intercutting. The actors are all pros which

helps, and we even get dependable Morris Ankrum doing a cameo as an autopsy surgeon.

The creatures, (there are two, an adult male and a young one), are outfitted in very good costumes, and have a unique look, not totally resembling the usual gorilla costume we are used to seeing, and they have slight human like features. The main ape man also shows it has a reasoning brain. All the more tragic is that between the stupid circus people kidnapping them and the so called science teams not being any help either, it's no wonder the adult monster goes berserk when its offspring is shot to death. He wipes out a native village nearby in retaliation, and ends up taking a volcano steam bath after being shot.

It cuts back and forth between the foreign production to John and his pals discussing the case. None of the Japanese scenes are dubbed into English. That's why John is there. He narrates. A lot. On the plus side, they actually have the monster suit of the child on the autopsy table for a prop which was apparently lent to them by Toho.

Fortunately the American scenes don't go on too long and just listening to Carradine talk can keep one entertained. It's so funny now in these older movies how everyone constantly lights up cigarettes, offering them to each other, putting out one and lighting up another like it's a fun hobby rather than a deadly habit. Some things do change for the better.

DICK TRACY MEETS GRUESOME

Dick Tracy faces the ruthless killer, Gruesome. If my mother named me Gruesome, I'd be a ruthless killer, too.

Oh, how I wish they had more of these Dick Tracy features. Yes, there are four serials, but the movies were nice little compact comic book stories. And the villains were all memorable; Gruesome being the best of them.

It's also too bad that Ralph Byrd didn't play Tracy in all the features; nothing against Morgan Conway, but after seeing Byrd in the serials, you couldn't imagine anyone else in role.

The great Boris Karloff plays the scowling gangster, Gruesome. This role gives the lie to the story about Boris not being right for the gangster role in *Black Friday*. Of course he could have played both the mild mannered professor and the cruel criminal, and Lugosi could have been moved up to Karloff's mad doctor role, making *Black Friday* a much better movie than it is. This role is even after *Black Friday* was made, so it's not that he grew too aged to pull it off. In any case, he's great here, with the toothpick in his mouth and monotone voice. He reminds one of how Bateman looked in *The Raven*, if he had two normal eyes. He's assisted by the one of the ugliest guys in Hollywood, Skelton Knaggs, whose pockmarked countenance exuded evil.

Byrd has a good rapport with his sidekick, Pat, played by Lyle Latell and the beautiful Anne Gwynne makes an appropriate Tess.

The gag in this one is the paralyzing gas, which makes it easy for Gruesome and the baddies to pull off bank jobs without interference. Initially Gruesome gets a whiff of the stuff and becomes a stiff himself. After he revives and waltzes out of the morgue, the screenwriters couldn't resist having Pat Patton make a reference to Gruesome reminding him of Boris Karloff. Such fun.

Kind of a nod to *Arsenic and Old Lace*?

WHAT A THREESOME! BORIS, OF COURSE, STRANGLING
RALPH BYRD, (THE BEST DICK TRACY PORTRAYER),
AND SKELTON KNAGGS, PROFESSIONAL UGLY GUY.

I LOVE A MYSTERY

Old time radio show gets both heard and seen.

To old time radio lovers, Carlton E. Morse's "I Love A Mystery" is one of the great radio serials. Each story featured three adventurers, Jack, Doc and Reggie. They solved murders, faced supernatural forces and got mixed up in just plain spooky stuff. It's too bad most of the serials are no longer intact; only two to my knowledge are complete. The one I like most is "Temple of Vampires". The cast changed over the years from the late 30's to the mid 40's, but of note is a young Tony Randall playing Reggie for a spell.

Columbia Pictures had the great idea to try a movie series based on the radio show. Their B movie unit ending up completing three movies, but apparently the series wasn't an audience grabber and they ceased production.

I guess Columbia thought three detectives was one too many, so they eliminated the character of Reggie. In the three films, Jack Packard was portrayed by Jim Bannon, and Doc was played by Barton Yardborough. Bannon appeared in the genre films *Soul of a Monster* and *Unknown World.* He was mostly prolific in appearing in TV westerns such as *Zorro, Lone Ranger, Wagon Train* and *Wyatt Earp.* Yarborough is known to Universal classic fans as the unfortunate Dr. Kettering in *Ghost of Frankenstein*, who is killed by the monster, (Lon Chaney), for no apparent reason other than he was there. His brain was supposed to be popped into the monster's skull, but old Ygor (Bela Lugosi) arranged a switcharoo with Dr. Bohmer played by Lionel "always willing to do the wrong thing" Atwill. Yarborough played Doc Long on the radio version for some years, and made the transition to television as Joe Friday's very first partner, Ben Romero in *Dragnet.*

The first entry simply titled *I Love a Mystery*, was graced by the presence of velvet voiced George McCready and Nina Foch. Foch is most remembered as Nicky in the underrated *Return of the Vampire*. She was also in the disappointing horror flick, *Cry of the Werewolf.*

McCready's character, Jefferson Monk, has an offer to sell his head to a weird cult after he dies, because of his resemblance to their leader from a thousand years ago. However, the cult doesn't want to wait, so a headless corpse shows up in the morgue. The series got off to a good start with the old pros at work being nasty. Another plus was all the movies had a film noir atmosphere.

The Devil's Mask was the next programmer and the one I feel is the most fun. You got it all in this one, voodoo, poison darts, shrunken heads, a panther on the loose and just to be consistent with the first movie, another headless body.

YOU CAN FIND EPISODES OF THE RADIO SHOW ONLINE AT SITES THAT SPECIALIZE IN OLD TIME RADIO PROGRAMS.

The Unknown was the last of the series and is more of an old dark house mystery. To me it seems like it could have been an episode on Boris Karloff's *Thriller* program. Set in an old mansion in the south, it keeps you guessing as to what exactly is going on. In the cast is James Bell who was a nutcase in *The Leopard Man*.

This would have been such a fun series to continue. You can catch the movies on Turner Classic Movies when they come around. Try them out.

CURSE OF THE DOLL PEOPLE

***If you go and steal an ancient idol, the doll people will come
and get you. Doesn't everyone know that?***

There have been a number of shrunken people movies; *Dr.
Cyclops, Attack of the Puppet People,* and the *Incredible Shrinking
Man* to name a few, but I've got to hand it to the Mexicans for
making the creepiest economy sized people I've ever seen.

They are actually animated dolls wearing the faces of their
victims. I can't tell if the people inside the suits are midgets or
children, but the head masks they wear, with that frozen look of
malevolence is what gives you the crawls. They are always silent
too which enhances the creep factor.

To top it off, we have an evil witch doctor and his zombie like
servant, who looks like he stepped out of the pages of an old *Tales
from the Crypt* comic book.

As usual with the K. Gordon Murray imports, the dubbing in
this one has the same florid and melodramatic renditions of the

dialog as all the others. It's even amusing to me now that I can identify the dubbing actors voices from film to film. I can hear one male voice in this and say, "Ah! That's the same guy that was the madman in *Samson in the Wax Museum*!" It makes the movies more endearing that way; like you're getting together with old friends.

I would have liked to see one of the other horror regulars in this one. It just isn't the same without Albert Salazar or German Robles.

It may be slow moving at times, but it is a pretty effective little flick. Just imagine one of these dolls walking into your bedroom one night and see if you don't feel "The Tingler" crawling up your back!

A BUCKET OF BLOOD

A would be sculptor discovers he works best when his models are plastered.

Dick Miller is one of those overlooked comic actors from the 50's. Even in a small part as the hipster vacuum cleaner salesman in *Not of This Earth*, he captures your interest while he's onscreen. The only place he didn't quite work for me was in *War of the Satellites*, where he was the nominal hero. "Normal" guy just doesn't fit him. This is his only starring role and he owns this movie.

Another black comedy in the vein of *Little Shop of Horrors*, this one skewers the pretentious art crowd and the beat movement of the 50's and early 60's.

Miller is the outsider among the outsiders, envying the cool arty types; wanting to be one of them, even though their talents are dubious.

The supporting cast is great. First we have Barboura Morris, one of my favorite actresses of the Corman crowd. We have

Anthony Carbone, who could be a stand in for Bogart and nearly was in *Creature From the Haunted Sea*. He was a frequent player in these Corman pictures, such as *Last Woman on Earth* and *Pit and thePendulum*. We also have a brief appearance by Ed Nelson, and a young Burt Convy, who ends up as a life size statue.

Initially we may feel sorry for Miller's character, Walter Paisley when he accidentally kills a cat trying to save it. The poor feline becomes his first art object and from then on, Walter has to kill again and again to keep his art career from crumbling. The scene where he cuts off a guy's head with a buzzsaw is all the more effective for not being shown. Today they would show you every last detail of that beheading. This is progress?

As I said, this is a black comedy, but if you roll with the murders, you're in for quite a grisly treat.

DEVIL GIRL FROM MARS

An imposing woman from Mars is looking for breeding stock for yet another planet devoid of males. When's that going to happen here?

Leather Girl from Mars would also be an appropriate title for this one, as the lead Martian, played by Patricia Laffan, looks like a fetishist dream.

Apparently Great Britain was competing against us for the planet of women genre. It was this one and *Fire Maidens from Outer Space* versus *Cat Women of the Moon* and *Queen of Outer Space*. With the exception of Fire Maidens they are all fun if you turn your brain off.

This movie benefits from the lovely presence of Hazel Court, who would come to more prominence in Hammer films and a couple of Roger Corman's Poe epics. She was sexy as hell and could play it for laughs such as in *The Raven*, or for evil such as in *Masque of the Red Death*. I remember her as well in a *Twilight Zone* episode about a giant alien terrorizing the countryside.

The plum role belongs to Laffan though, who looks about eight feet tall, with a black leather helmut, black short leather tunic and with eyebrows rivaling *The Astounding She Monster.* Unlike the She Monster though, she talks, and you'd better listen!

Accompanying her is a big bulky robot, sort of like Gort if he ate too many Twinkies. It's somewhat reminiscent of the boxy looking robots from old Republic serials except wider. It's imposing in its tank like dimensions, but you don't see it often enough. The space ship is pretty cool, too.

Like a lot of British films, it's very talky, but if you're hanging out late at night in front of the set, it's a fun enough diversion. The script was actually based on a play which I would have paid big bucks to see.

"DOES THIS OUTFIT MAKE ME LOOK FAT?"

BRIDE OF THE MONSTER

A crazed scientist wants to create a race of supermen in his basement. Every boy's dream.

Fasten your seat belts, we're about to enter Ed Wood land where anything can happen!

It's amazing to think that so many movies are considered classics because of their excellence, but two Ed Wood movies, this one, and Plan 9 are also classics but for a different reason.

Say what you will about Wood, he certainly had a distinct directing style or lack thereof, and his scripts seem like they were translated from a foreign language. But they are so damned enjoyable, you can watch them again and again, unlike many conventional classics.

Although Plan 9 is probably everyone's favorite Wood film, Bride is his most accessible movie. It's more like a real movie. This is Lugosi's last speaking role, and even though he's on his last legs, as usual he gives it his all and is even touching in his "I have no home," monologue.

The huge icing on the cake is Tor Johnson, as much a cult icon as Rondo Hatton, as he plays Lobo for the first time. He was Lobo in *The Unearthly* and in *Night of the Ghouls* as well.

The rest of the cast is a mixed bag. Tony McCoy, the lead male, is pretty wooden but I'm assuming he wasn't really actor material in the first place, just a bone thrown to his father who put money into the movie. A strange characterization is delivered by Harvey B. Dunn, of *Teenagers from Outer Space*, who is the oddest police captain I've ever seen, with a parakeet on his shoulder through most it. Maybe the parakeet was the brains behind the police station, "Bwwak, he's lying! He's lying! Arrest him! Bwakk!"

The other lead is better, played by Loretta King.

Apparently there was a major battle between her and Dolores Fuller, who assumed she had the lead and then got dumped down to a cameo. (Which is really where she belonged at all times.)

We even see Billy Benedict, one of the last of the Bowery Boys, stick his head in the door for a while.

Paul Marco makes his debut as Kelton the cop providing a kind of comedy relief known only to him.

Then we have the octopus. Wherever they got it, borrowed it, stole it, asked for it, etc., the fact that it's an inert object doesn't exactly help the stunt man who gets killed by it at the end. It's reminiscent of *The Creeping Terror* where the victims had to voluntarily climb into the monster's mouth. In this one, the poor guy had to wrap the tentacles around him and struggle with the limp appendages.

Now if Dr. Vornoff got his way and created a race of supermen, one by one, it would probably have taken him about a century or so to find enough subjects that lived through his experiment. I don't think he could have lasted that long, unless Lobo would have taken over for him.

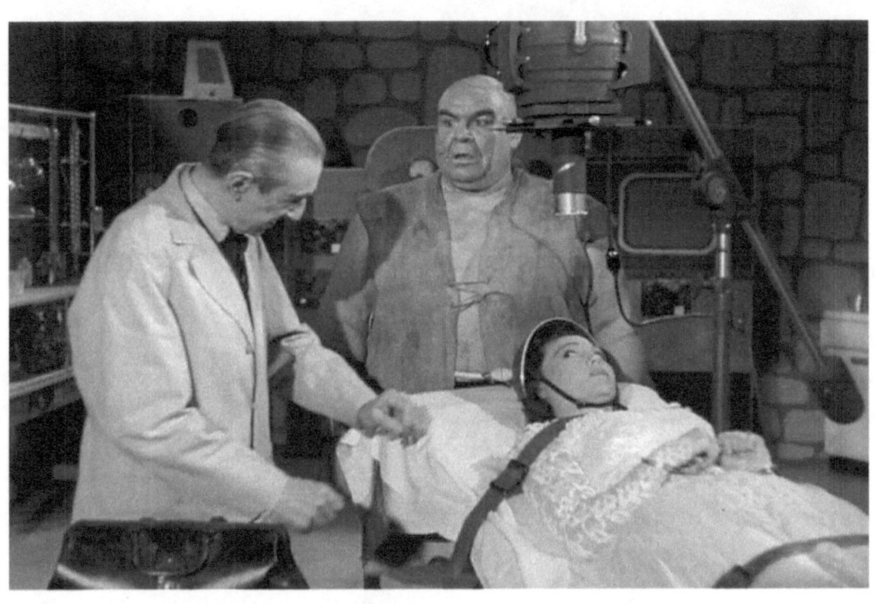

**TOR AND BELA MAKE A GREAT COMEDY
TEAM IN THIS MOVIE.**

CASTLE OF THE LIVING DEAD

A crazy count indulges his hobby of taxidermy on a visiting actor's troupe.

Like Barbara Steele, Christopher Lee made quite a few horror movies in Italy. Fortunately this is one where he dubbed his own voice, unlike most of the others.

At first Lee seems like he might be undead himself, considering his pale face and dark rings around his eyes, but he isn't. He's just bug nutty.

He has some kind of formula that freezes people in place; I'm assuming they die that way but it's hard to say. In any case, when the count has a chance to have a permanent acting troupe in his castle, he starts to collect them one by one. Hopefully there's a play called "Still Life" they can enact.

Lee is somber throughout, as if he's stuffed himself, except in a scene which for some reason amuses me. The actors portray a comic hangman scene, (no, not the spelling kind), and Lee laughs raucously and applauds this morbid tableau. A real fun guy, this count.

A young Donald Sutherland appears in a dual role in this movie. For some reason he's in drag as an old woman with the voice dubbed, but he's mostly a kind of comic relief as a dim witted policeman. He also dubbed his own voice. Later on in life, Sutherland would share a railroad car with Lee in *Dr. Terror's House of Horrors*.

One scene that shocked me when I first saw it as a kid is when one of the burly members of the troupe get shot in the eye with one of Lee's paralyzing darts. Bullseye.

Of course, Lee gets his comeuppance at the end, when he gets on the receiving end of one his darts.

I wonder what they did afterward with all those frozen human beings?

"HI, I'M DON, AND THESE ARE ASSISTANTS, MOE AND LARRY."

Two scientists thaw out an ape man. I can't believe I just wrote that.

The last of the Monogram features has Lugosi and Carradine together again, and depending who you ask, briefly with George Zucco.

That is actually the most intriguing aspect of this movie. Zucco was supposed to play the ape man, and at the very least was featured in publicity stills. Whether he actually ended up in the final cut is open to debate. I know I have looked for him even if it's only a brief glimpse, but I confess I've yet to spot him. It's kind of like looking for a hairy Where's Waldo? Zucco bowed out of the production supposedly because of illness, but it could have been the role that made him sick. He was replaced by Monogram regular Frank Moran, who is the one I always see in the movie.

I think Lugosi is the most evil I've seen him in a Monogram. There's usually some kind of softness in his other Monograms, but in the two Ape Man movies, he has no redeeming characteristics.

This is NOT a sequel to The Ape Man; the return refers to Lugosi and Carradine bringing their ape-sicle home and defrosting him. Then Bela gets the bright idea of putting a human brain in the ape man. Unluckily for John's character, it's his brain that will be making the swap.The great thing about being a mad scientist is you don't have to have a very good reason to do anything. Just do it.

Carradine is very subdued in this one; maybe his heart wasn't in it because later on his brain would be. In any case you miss those Carradine eyes flashing or the deep intonations.

Bela's best line in the movie is in the party scene, when he is contemplating whose brain to use in his experiment. Observing the party guests he says with his usual jocularity, "You know, some peoples brains would never be missed!" Bela, you'd have a whole bunch of people to choose from nowadays.

After Carradine's character makes the brain switch, the Carradine/Ape man wanders upstairs and plays the piano, a talent his human self had. Then his wife walks in and he turns on her in a New York minute and murders her. Talk about moody.

It's a hard contest to choose which is the most bizarre Lugosi Monogram movie, but for me it's between this one and Black Dragons.

I think this movie could have used Mantan Moreland in it.

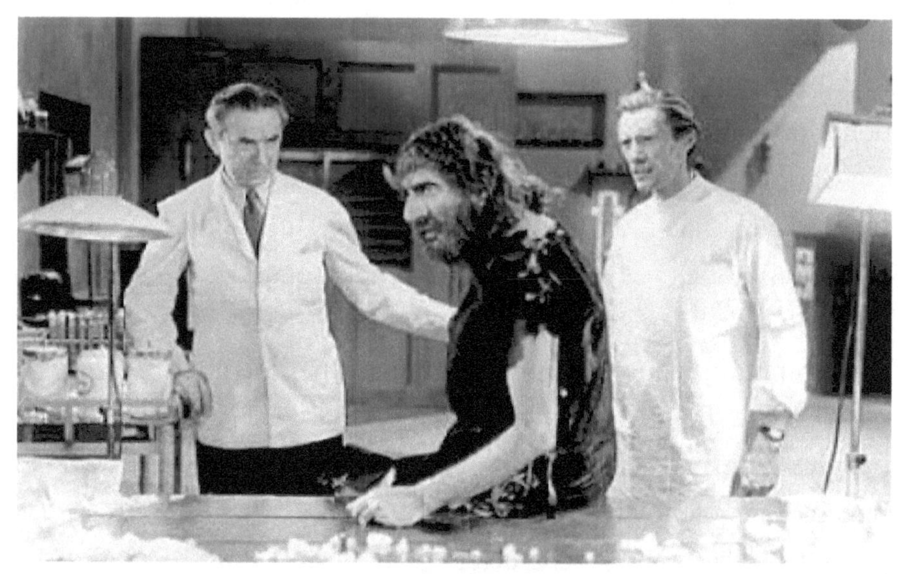

THE ONLY PHOTO OF GEORGE ZUCCO AS THE APE MAN. WHETHER ANY FOOTAGE OF HIM WAS EVER SHOT IS OPEN TO DEBATE.

I BURY THE LIVING

A cemetery keeper thinks he's bumping people off when he puts a black pin on the cemetery map.

I have mixed feelings about this movie. It's a very well done and atmospheric movie, and Richard Boone has a juicy role, but the juice of the movie itself runs dry at the end.

Richard Boone is the unwilling custodian of a cemetery who slowly gets dragged into a nightmare when he thinks he may have the power of life and death. White pins on the cemetery map represent the living who have reserved their final resting place, and the black pins are those who have already checked in. When Boone's character accidentally puts a black pin on the map of someone still alive, they suddenly die and we're off and running.

Assisting him is Andy, played by folk singer, Theodore Bikel, who is a chiseler. I mean, he chisels the names on the gravestones.

So much is spooky here. The cemetery itself gives you creeps. The map on the wall seems like a living, breathing entity. Bikel looks rather threatening in some vague way. Boone, who feels he is losing his grip on reality, gives a great performance of a man who starts to believe he has the power of life and death.

Near the end, feeling responsible for the deaths he thinks he's caused, Boone replaces black pins with white ones, thinking he can raise the dead. Sure enough, he finds a lot of empty graves and assumes the corpses have gone on strike. We're expecting at this point to see a lot of dead people walking around but here's where it comes crashing down. Andy, the assistant, was bumping off people to get even with being dismissed from his job after 40 years. He managed to unbury all those people in record time while the cops watched him. What he hoped to accomplish by digging people up is anyone's guess, but it was enough to kill him from exhaustion.

I've read that the original script called for a supernatural explanation, but for some dumb reason, the producer nixed it. What a classic spook show this would have been if not for that bone headed mistake. As it is, it's still worth watching until it runs off the rails in the finale.

I would think that Bikel's character could have easily started a new career as the world's fastest grave digger instead of going through all this other trouble. He needed a career counselor.

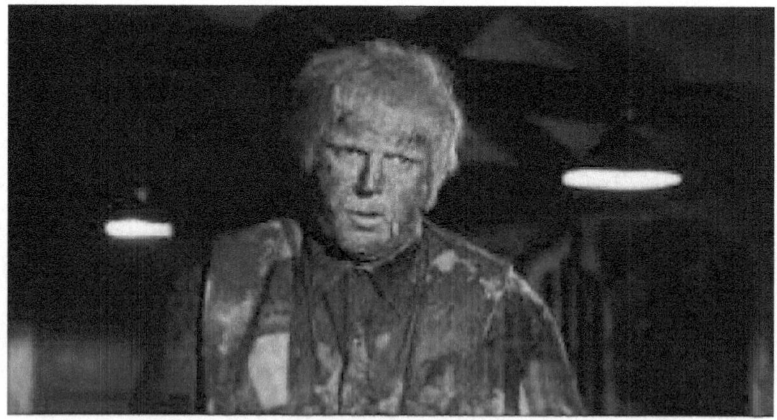

"YOU'D BE TIRED TOO IF YOU DUG UP SIX GRAVES IN FIVE MINUTES!"

THE INDESTRUCTIBLE MAN

Butcher Benton vows revenge on the crooks that double crossed him, but he has to be dead first before he can do that.

I first saw this on Fantasmic Features on my local Boston station. The horror host of my youth was a little space alien named Feep and he showed a lot of the Allied Artists B's. I wondered why it seemingly started midway through the movie. It was the part where Bob Shayne tries to inject Chaney with a hypo and it bends on his skin. Just like Superman. It wasn't till later that I found out that the TV prints had to be padded with a preview scene, then a long crawl of prologue gibberish. In some cases they double printed frames of the movie in certain sections so the action looked choppy. All to fit a time slot more snugly.

At any rate, this is a Chaney showcase, even though he only speaks briefly at the beginning. Because the movie was shot on locations, it's a little disconcerting to see Chaney walking down the sidewalk with pedestrians looking at him. Chaney comes back to life and gets revenge on the people who double crossed him. Throwing them off buildings seems like a good idea to him. Let someone else clean up the mess. Of course, by the end, Chaney is a mess himself, being burned up, both literally and figuratively. Casey Adams, (the actual first Ward Cleaver in the pilot show of Leave It To Beaver), is the wholesome cop. I think they wanted his voice more than him, because he narrates a lot and sounds a little like Jack Webb. The stripper seems wholesome too, but then again, everyone looks wholesome next to Chaney in this one. I think Charlie Manson would look wholesome.

"I CAN'T TELL. ARE YOU IN JAIL OR AM I?"

THE AMAZING TRANSPARENT MAN

A nutcase army major wants to use another criminal for his invisibility ray. Good plan.

Edgar Ulmer was busy during the 50's doing low budget epics like this one, *Beyond the Time Barrier* and *Daughter of Dr. Jekyll*. He had come down a long way from his brilliant and disturbing *The Black Cat* at Universal. He gets to tackle an invisible man premise with variable results.

Douglas Kennedy is the transparent man, an escaped con named Faust, (how appropriate), who is sprung by by a former army man, Maj. Paul Krenner. Krenner is putting the screws to a scientist by stashing away his daughter. He wants to use Faust to steal valuable radium, so he figures an invisible man can accomplish that rather easily. Once he has everything he needs, he can create an invisible army. As Tears for Fears said it in song, "Everybody Wants to Rule the World." I could never figure out why anyone would want to rule the entire world. First of all, it's physically impossible, so you need underlings to represent you all over the world. How many underlings does it take to screw in a lightbulb? None. They're too busy robbing you blind while you're not around.

The effects are minimal, although I liked the scene when Faust is first made invisible while lying on the table. He screams as he fades away and I thought that was different and cool. Sorry, no great matte effects with empty clothes here, just a bunch of wire rigged props moving about by themselves.

Major Krenner is played by James Griffith, who doesn't seem right in this part to me. I think it needed someone with more of a bulldozer personality. Actually he and Kennedy could have switched parts and I think it would have worked better. I will say Griffith is good at thrashing around pretending to be strangled by an invisible man. Griffith has been seen in better things, especially one of the best *Thriller* episodes, "Parasite Mansion." He was also the strange lab assistant who dies at the hands of John Beal in *The Vampire*. I don't see the usefulness of an invisible army. The trouble with an invisible army is you never know when any of the soldiers are making faces at you.

Douglas Kennedy almost always played a heavy; the only time I can think of him being a good guy was a small part he had in *The Alligator People*. Usually he was seen on TV shows as a bad cop, criminal or other low life.

At the end, the elderly scientist who invented the invisibility ray, (who looks like he could be Eduardo Ciannelli's brother), breaks the fourth wall and addresses the audience when asked if some inventions should not be made available to the military. "What would you do?" he asks. What, indeed?

The whole thing goes by in an hour, so if you want to see every movie concerning an invisible man, you can see this one.

I often wonder what would have happened to Edgar Ulmer if he hadn't fallen from grace with Universal Pictures. He certainly created a classic with *The Black Cat*. If he had stayed would he have directed other Universal horrors down the line? I wonder how his version of *House of Frankenstein* or *Frankenstein Meets the Wolf Man* would have looked?

THE BAT

The classic thriller is brought to the screen for the third time. Batter up!

Mary Roberts Rhinehart's mystery thriller has been around a long time. It was a play, a novel, a silent movie, a sound movie titled *The Bat Whispers*, and this last version which is graced by the presence of Vincent Price and Agnes Morehead.

Morehead makes a grand detective fiction writer and has the right amount of level headedness and inquisitiveness to sell the role. Vincent Price is here to serve as a red bat, I mean, herring, but just having Vinnie around gives extra class to the movie that it might not have had otherwise.

Each version is a little different from the book/play, mostly in simplification, but I find both sound versions quite enjoyable. I saw pictures of this one in either *Horror Monsters* or *Mad Monsters* magazine, and it was quite a while before I got to see the movie. Nicely shot, it has a cool twangy theme for the Bat himself.

Darla Hood of Our Gang is here, all grown up, and lasts long enough to be a victim. This seems to be her biggest role in a feature, but she did do bits in other films and appeared in several TV shows of the era. I also get a kick out seeing the policeman played by none other than Gavin Gordon, who way back in 1935 played Lord Byron in the prologue of *Bride of Frankenstein*. Also on board is John Sutton who was the scientist who made Vincent Price invisible in *The Invisible Man Returns*.

It helps if you don't know the outcome, but I don't think you'd be reading this book if you hadn't already seen the movie.

"NEXT I'M GOING TO MAKE A LITTLE DOGGIE."

THE KILLER SHREWS

These shrews are very hard to tame.

I first saw this movie when it came out in the theaters, and to show you how old memories can be faulty, I remembered it being in color. It wasn't until later on that I discovered that it was a black-and-white movie. For me this is a fun and unusual movie. I do remember when I was little I could still tell that the shrews were actually dogs in shaggy coats, but that didn't bother me much. What is chilling is not their appearance, but the sound they make. I wouldn't want to hear that sound coming from my basement, I'll tell you that. James Best is the hero in this movie and he was always a good character actor who was very busy in the 50s and 60s. He could play a good guy or a bad guy and get away with it. If you want to see him in full throttle as a loony, catch him in the movie, *Shock Corridor.* The movie is interesting to me because it takes what is an otherwise harmless little animal and makes it a frightening one by having them grow to doggie size. The latter part of the movie may remind you of *Night of the Living Dead* as the survivors are barricaded in the house trying to keep the shrews from breaking in. The rest of the cast is adequate but the standout bad guy is played by Ken Curtis, who later played Festus on *Gunsmoke*. He's a weasel and a coward and he gets what he deserves; being lunch for the shrews. Many people find humorous the way the survivors get away from the shrews by getting under large metal barrels and duck walking their way to the shore. It may look silly but it saves their lives and actually make sense as a protection against shrews. If my life was in danger I'd wear a chicken outfit if it would save me. The shrews are most effective when a puppet head and lower torso are used. The big long teeth and the nasty look on the face is pretty chilling. The puppet is very effective in the gruesome basement scene. The shrews work best when they're gnawing through the walls, their snouts sticking in

"HELLO, I'M THE LOCAL BUILDING INSPECTOR."

the holes they make, coupled with the creepy sound of their chatter. The primary weakness is using dogs as the shrews. It would've been passable if the dog/shrews were shown only in a long shot such as coming over the horizon. It's when they're shown in a medium shot that it becomes all too obvious that they're canines with shaggy coats.

All in all this movie doesn't deserve the bad reputation it has. I think in spite of the low budget, it is still an enjoyable movie.

SPIDER BABY

When Lon Chaney is the sanest one in the cast, you know you're in trouble.

If you go by this movie's various titles, you might not think that this is a very black comedy. But it is, and it's one of the weirdest ones ever.

Lon Chaney has the last great role of his career as a sympathetic caretaker to a family that has some kind of genetic disease where they devolve into cannibalism.

When greedy relatives make the scene, the truth comes out and the family unit, such as it is, literally blows up.

Jack Hill directed this opus, and Chaney was reportedly on his good behavior alcohol wise until the very end. He is funny, touching, caring and never once threatening through the entire movie, and it's a pleasure to watch him when he knows he's doing something worthwhile. He even sends up his Wolf Man character in a dinner scene that resembles a Norman Rockwell painting as envisioned by Alice Cooper.

The cast is something else. Mantan Moreland, savior of many a Monogram movie, has a brief bit here as a doomed delivery man. I wish they hadn't killed him though; I could imagine a running joke of Moreland constantly having to come back to the house and deliver packages of questionable items. At least someone gave him work at the end of his career.

Beverly Washburn and Jill Banner are the demonic duo is this one. Washburn has her nice girl persona mostly, which makes it all the more terrifying when her face transforms into a bloodthirsty grimace. Banner is a strikingly beautiful young girl with the soul of a butcher. Sid Haig perfectly embodies a childlike goon and is scary in a quiet, drooling way.

It's good to see Carol Ohmart again as one of the greedy relatives. The only other film I've seen her in was *House on Haunted Hill*. She goes downhill mentally in a big way by the end of this film.

"SO REMEMBER, NOT EVERYONE IS AS NICE AS WE ARE."

Look at this movie with a Addams Family point of view and you'll be fine. Look at it seriously and you may go to bed that night seriously disturbed.

CREATURE FROM THE HAUNTED SEA

A mythical sea monster makes itself known to a gang of criminals. And is it a sight to behold!

These early Roger Corman films are an inspiration to all low budget/no budget film makers of today. Movies like this one and *Little Shop of Horrors* were knocked off quickly and cheaply and it's the cheapness of them that make them so lovable. It helps too that they're comedies which excuses any lapse of quality in my eyes. Robert Towne, before he became a famed screenwriter for *Chinatown* and others, plays the most inept, uncharismatic hero I've ever seen. He is so bad at being cool, he couldn't make ice cubes in Alaska. Betsy Jones-Moreland, looking good in her one piece bathing suit, is visibly disgusted by his advances and who wouldn't be? Then we have Anthony Carbone, who seems like a stand in for Bogart in *Key Largo*, a ship's mate who makes animal noises, and the most wonderfully goofy looking monster. He looks kind of like a happy Baby Ruth bar.

This is probably the most far out of the Corman quickie comedies, bordering on surrealistic. We have Cuban refugees who have absconded with the country's treasury after a coup, a large islander female who falls for the animal imitator played by Beach Dickerson, a pay phone in the middle of nowhere, lots of silly spy stuff at the beginning; it's just plain delirious.

The first time I saw this movie, I was young and didn't know how to take it. Now I get a big kick out of the absurdity of the whole thing. If you let yourself, you will too.

PHANTOM FROM SPACE

An alien crash lands on earth and scares people by wearing Robot Monster's helmet. Things don't get better for him when he removes it. He's invisible.

Some of the first movies I remember seeing as a tyke on local creature feature shows were all from director Lee Wilder. They are all universally trashed, and not without reason; they tend to be talky and dull, but I still hold a fondness for them. *Snow Creature* gave us the first Yeti movie, *Killers from Space* gave us those iconic pop eyed aliens and this one may be the first invisible invader, pre-dating the Id monster of *Forbidden Planet* and *Invisible Invaders*, a John Agar fave of mine.

You got to give the guy credit for that anyway.

I think this is his best feature, since it has some effective scenes and the fact that the alien really isn't evil so you kind of feel sorry for him at the end.

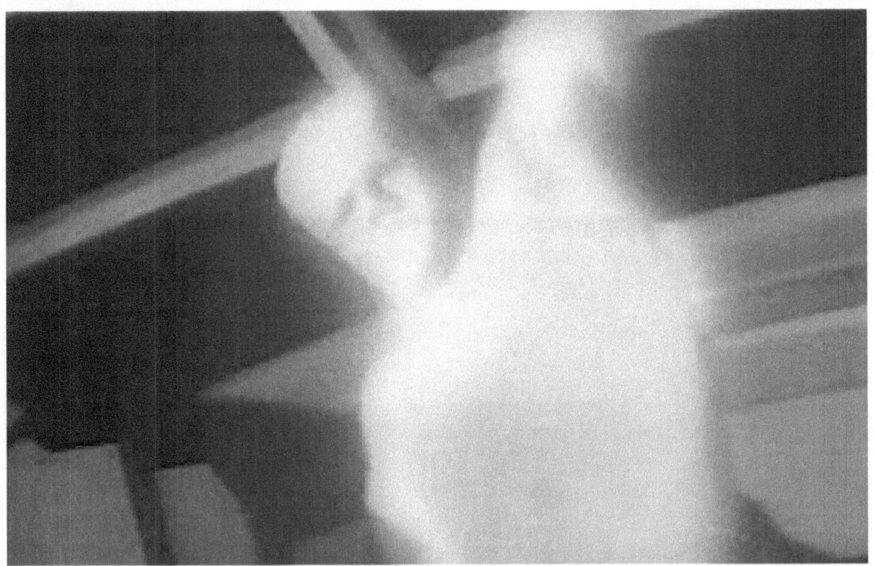

There are no really recognizable faces in this one, other than Rudolph Anders, (*She Demons*), and Michael Mark, (*Wasp Woman*, and a regular face in Universal Classics.)

The first chunk is taken up by narration which makes one fear another *Creeping Terror* movie, but it snaps out of that. The scenes of the phantom trying to communicate via tapping scissors on a table, and a pretty decent shot of an invisible man picking up the woman, add a little pizzaz to it.

The alien, who is never seen as clearly as in the photos, looks something like a more placid version of the *The Thing*, but his spacesuit seems to consist of a bathing suit and nothing else.

Typical drive in fare, which is why we showed it on one of our drive in shows. Have some popcorn and soda nearby and give this one a look.

FACE OF MARBLE

Two scientists experiment with a way to raise the dead. Weird stuff follows.

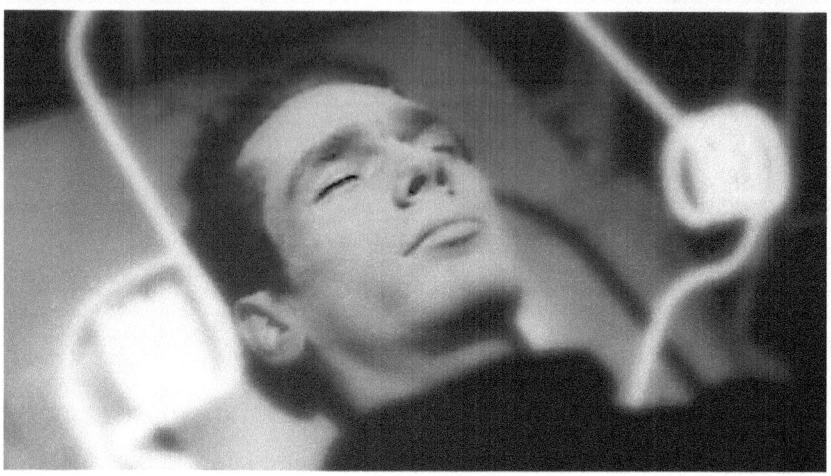

John Carradine is back, courtesy of Monogram Studios! This movie has always been a disappointment to me, because it had the potential to be another cool zombie film. There was also a misleading publicity still of a revived corpse grabbing Carradine by the neck, which never happens in the film.

Carradine and Robert Shayne, (Shayne practicing to raise Lon Chaney from the dead in *The Indestructible Man*), have a device to raise the dead, or least make them turn over on their side. The first subject is a dead sailor, and initially it looks like it might be successful. The face of the dead man turns white. The docs proclaim it has a "face of marble" which sounds better than a "face of Formica". The guy opens his eyes, but quickly goes back to the big sleep. This is probably the best scene of the picture and then it goes off on a different tangent. We have a ghost dog. We have Willie Best standing in for Mantan Moreland. Best was a more embarrassing stereotype and it tends to overshadow the fact that he was a good comic actor. The lead woman also undergoes the *Face of Marble* challenge. A voodoo priestess gets into the game. The police show up. Really, you need a scorecard to keep track.

The movie doesn't know what it wants to be and seems thrown together. They should have stuck to one theme. I vote for the zombie theme, but we could have had a voodoo theme too.

Carradine is restrained in this one and he's not offset by Shayne who acts about the same. One of them should have been bug nutty. It would have added something to it. I believe this was the last Monogram horror film of the forties. I think they just wanted to shove this one out the door and forget it.

You can make a drinking game with this film. Every time John Carradine calls Robert Shayne, "my boy", take a shot. The irony is that Shayne was older than Carradine in real life.

HERE'S THE ULTIMATE DISHONEST PUBLICITY PHOTO. THE GUY NEVER GETS OFF THE TABLE IN THE MOVIE.

THE CORPSE VANISHES

Bela is at it again, this time trying to keep his wife happy.

Abandon logic, all ye who enter here. You are now entering Monogram land, where you start a story with an outlandish premise, then figure out the absolute worst way to achieve your objective. Add Bela Lugosi to it and you have a helluva fun ride.

I would have loved to be a screenwriter for Monogram's horror flicks. You didn't have to worry about things making sense, you just wrote whatever wild idea came to mind. You knew you were writing something that would just be goofy and entertaining. You didn't have your eyes on an Oscar.

The people that slam these cheapies simply don't understand the conditions under which they were made. They're assuming that all film companies wanted to put out movies that had lasting worth, would engage the audience in its intelligent wordplay and would make a film that lingers in the mind long afterward. Well, they're wrong. These people knew what they were doing. They were churning out quickies to fill the bill for the bigger A pictures. They were the bubble gum to chew on before you got to the steak. But aha! History has a way of throwing you a curve. Frequently, wacky movies like this linger in the mind far longer than many of the A movies that have been largely forgotten. Why? Because they are fun to watch! They weren't meant to be taken seriously as great art. These old B's, along with the serials of the day, have a tremendous influence on today's extravaganzas. *Star Wars*? C'mon! Its Flash Gordon with a huge bank account. Indiana Jones is a mix of every old serial you've never seen. *Jaws* and *Alien* are just old fashioned monster flicks. Yet people trash these cheap predecessors because they didn't have ton of money behind them. Give it a rest, willya?

The Corpse Vanishes is a delirious Lugosi vehicle and with Bela behind the wheel it's bound to go the wrong way on the off ramp. Bela's wife, played by Elizabeth Russell, really hates the idea of getting old, so Bela has a way to cure that. Just get some glandular fluid from young women and inject it into his selfish

"HERE, LET ME BUTTON THAT TOP BUTTON."

wife.   Believe me, she doesn't deserve it. She's nasty and unfeeling. I don't know what Bela sees in her.

So even granted that the serum works, Bela goes through the trouble of kidnapping brides at the altar after they inhale a drugged orchid. Talk about drawing attention to yourself. He's helped in his endeavor by a dwarf, (the ever present Angelo Rossitto), a half wit and his sister, (again played by Minerva Urecal, who apparently didn't learn anything from The Ape Man).

Luanna Walters and Tristan Coffin, faces you'd know from old serials are also on hand for the festivities.

Bela makes no effort to shield his weirdness. When visitors come to call, they see the coffins that he and his wife sleep in. Bela explains how comfortable they are and that many people sleep in coffins. I've yet to meet one, Bela, sorry.

BEAST OF YUCCA FLATS

A large Russian scientist gets caught in a blast and reverts to a mindless primitive. And he needs a new wardrobe.

Considering all the trash talk aimed at these movies, so many icons that permeate our culture today came from these humble B movies. Rondo Hatton's face, the She Creature, the Saucermen, Robot Monster, etc, but Tor Johnson became such an idol of fans that the Don Post studios made a mask of him. How many big time Hollywood stars can say that?

Tor didn't need to speak; indeed, he was better off silent because his heavy accent made a lot of his dialog in Plan 9 hard to understand. However, he did know how to look and act scary, which I assume came from his wrestling days.

This is the probably the only time he starred in a movie and he is in it throughout. Again, it's another movie I only saw pictures of in *Horror Monsters* magazine for the longest time, but I finally got to see it via a VHS copy from Sinister Cinema.

Here we go again. Another mostly narrated movie. Was this some kind of fad, or just a bunch of coincidences? One thing I can say, the narration in this movie is way out, man, I mean, I'm hep, I'm with it, I mean…whadz he mean?

I think if you took the narration from this movie and printed it in the book as beat poetry, people would buy it.

Here's just some of them courtesy of the IMDB:

Flag on the moon. How did it get there?

Touch a button. Things happen. A scientist becomes a beast.

Nothing bothers some people, not even flying saucers.

Twenty hours without rest and still no enemy. In the blistering desert heat, Jim and Joe plan their next attack. Find the Beast and kill him. Kill, or be killed. Man's inhumanity to man.

Everyone once in a while, some dubbing occurs when a character is turned away from the camera, which helps a little, but not much.

Much of the film is shot outdoors which I imagine saved time and money. There are no special effects to speak of, other than Tor's burned face makeup.

The movie runs about an hour but somewhere along the line it had a new sequence added to the beginning that features a topless woman being killed by someone? Who? Tor isn't a monster until later. And who added this scene? The director, Coleman Francis?

Tor Johnson? (I think Tor could have made a better movie, actually.)

"TOR PUT NEW SWIMMING POOL HERE!"

I would say that the monster boom generation was seeded about 1957. That's when American International, Allied Artists and other studios started churning out sci-fi and horror movies geared to a teenage crowd. The famed Shock Theater package of Universal classics were released to TV and the first generation of monster crazed kids took hold.

Something else that took hold was our fascination with the printed page, and the magazines that kindled our interest in scary cinema.

The top tier studios such as MGM, 20th Century Fox, Warner Brothers, Columbia and Universal were offset by the bottom tier studios of Monogram, PRC and Republic, known as "poverty row." These small studios turned out product fast and cheap and even occasionally rented out the sets from the big studios.

There was a similar situation in the magazine field. *Famous Monsters of Filmland* was first published in 1958, and what was initially conceived as a one shot publication became an unexpected success. Other companies took note and soon other magazines flooded the drugstore racks, some lasting only one issue, others going for a half a dozen or so. The competitor to FM was *Castle of Frankenstein*, which was aimed at a more mature audience of readers and carried on into the 1970s before suddenly disappearing. Other notables appeared briefly such as *Fantastic Monsters of the Films, Monster Mania and Modern Monster*s.

I have a huge fondness for what I would call the poverty row of monster magazines: *Mad Monsters* and *Horror Monsters*. These two magazines were published by Charlton Comics, mainly a publisher of what would be considered lower grade comics books.

I don't know what it is: the fact that they were published in New England where I live, that they were some of the first magazines I ever collected, their great colorful covers, I just don't know, but whenever I flip through an old issue I get much more of a nostalgic feeling than I get from old FMs.

They were printed on cheap newspaper stock, so the photo reproductions were pretty spotty. The two magazines were also a bit of a mess editorially; they were half humorous, half serious, and half publicity machines for whatever studio would give them materials to print.

The humor articles ran the gamut from out and out old Mad Magazine type comic stories drawn by some unknown Charlton artist, to pun laden articles which would even embarrass Forry Ackerman. I liked the funny photo captions page the best, although I didn't know what movies some of them were from.

On the more serious side, they did manage some good interviews with Bob Burns and Glenn Strange. One of my fondest memories was their version of a film book. Of course, FM had their own film books which would give you the complete synopsis of a movie along with a great gallery of stills. What Mad/Horror Monsters did was a little different. Along with the standard stills, you not only got the movie told in story form, you got virtually all the dialog spoken in the movie on the printed page. For a kid in the pre-VHS era, this was almost as good as seeing it on TV. I could re-experience Invasion of the Body Snatchers, Frankenstein Meets the Wolf Man and House of Frankenstein. By the time I saw the movies again, I could repeat the dialog with them, they became so engrained.

In those magazines I also saw pictures of movies I had yet to see: *Black Zoo, The Bat, Beast of Yucca Flats, Return of Dracula,*

Valley of the Dragons, Tales of Terror, Spiderwoman Strikes Back and many others.

I don't know if it was from embarrassment or not, but the editors would never use their real name on the credits page. "Abernathy Farquad" may always be a mystery as to who sported that name.

Both of the magazines lasted ten issues, which was longer than a lot of the other fly by night rivals. To those of us who were able to pick up copies of them, they are a cherished part of our childhood. The poverty row of magazines is still solid gold to me.

STRANGLER OF THE SWAMP

A vengeful ghost knocks off the descendants of those who hanged him. He's probably also angry that he's stuck in a swamp for eternity.

I would never want Charles Middleton angry at me. I've seen the way he acted as Ming the Merciless in the old Flash Gordon serials. He'd be even worse as a ghost.

Actually, if you could hear a ghost speak I think it would sound like Charles Middleton, even a female ghost. There is something so ominous and threatening in his voice that I wouldn't even buy ice cream from him.

Some people have argued that the ghost would have been more effective if it were silent, and I might agree if it were some other actor, but this is Charles Middleton, come on! You can't waste that voice. Add that to the creepy way he looks and you can't lose.

PRC rises above its threadbare budget with this one. They make good use of the fog effects which masks the smallness of the sets. Between that, the darkness and the craggy trees littering the landscape, you have one atmospheric film.

The cast is decent as well. Rosemary La Planche does a creditable job in the lead as the ferry woman who gets to meet with

Charlie during a crossing on the swamp. She almost sacrifices herself in order to stop the ghost from killing. I found it rather touching when Middleton "gives up the ghost" at the end, due to her willingly offering her life to him.

Blake Edwards, yes, that Blake Edwards is the good guy type, but I'm glad he stopped acting and produced the great Peter Sellers Pink Panther movies instead.

Yeah, it can be slow moving at times, but the pluses outweigh the minuses. And did I mention that Charles Middleton is the ghost?

MOST DANGEROUS GAME

A madman hunts human beings for sport on his remote island. Unfortunately, Gilligan isn't one of the targets.

Richard Connell's classic short story has been adapted a few times to the silver screen, but this first version is by far the best of them all.

It's hard to believe that *King Kong* was being worked on at the same time as this picture, in terms of the effects, but we get to see some of that cast getting in on this "game" as well. The beautiful Fay Wray, along with Robert Armstrong and Noble Johnson from the Kong cast are joined by hero Joel McCrea and British actor Leslie Banks.

So, all public domain movies must be bad, right? WRONG! This is a great film, and should rate high on anyone's list. It's akin to getting on a roller coaster. You feel the anticipation as you climb the hill, then you're over the bend and down you go and never stop.

Poor Fay is again the rather bedraggled heroine, but she still shows the stuff she's made of as she keeps up with McCrea as they rush frantically through the jungle. And boy, that jungle looks familiar. It should. It's Kong's jungle which they used for this movie as well. I can recognize Kong's felled tree where he had a log rolling contest with some hapless sailors. (How fun would it have been if Wray and McCrea fell into the spider pit and we got to see the critters this time?)

Oh well, no time to play with giant arachnids anyway, not with wild eyed Banks chasing you with Noble Johnson and slavering dogs.

I appreciate the part where McCrea's character, who is a hunter himself, admits he now knows how the animals must feel when he hunted them. Hunting just for sport is appalling to me, and I liked that acknowledgement in so old a film.

Banks was rarely in USA films, but he was also a baddie in *Chamber of Horrors*, which I also ran on my show.

Robert Armstrong is soooo different from the cocky Carl Denham in this one. He's a loose goose drunk who ends up a trophy. I've seen stills from this movie that don't appear in the film and I swear that somewhere I saw a still of Robert Armstrong's head on the trophy wall.

Noble Johnson is almost unrecognizable here as a Russian henchmen, with his pale skin and beard. It's one of the two times that this black actor was made up as white man, the other being *Murders in the Rue Morgue*. He's one of the those people that can be threatening without saying a word.

See this movie if you like fast moving thrillers. What more can I say?

"THAT'S THE SECOND WEIRDEST ICE CUBE I'VE EVER SEEN!"

Oh, Bela, women are nothing but trouble for you, aren't they?

I guess you can say it's a ghost since Bela is haunted by his first wife who ran off and supposedly got killed in a car crash. What Bela doesn't know is that she didn't die, she just lost her mind, and the servants are keeping her locked up on the grounds in secret.

It's a Monogram movie! Instead of simply letting Bela know his wife survived so he could decide whether to patch things up with her or divorce her, they hide her so he thinks she's dead. Then when she escapes and Bela sees her standing outside from his window, does Bela tell anyone what he saw? No, he loses his mind as well, and turns into a homicidal killer. Monogram rule of thumb: do things in the worst ways imaginable. But if they did things sanely, we wouldn't have another full throttle Lugosi performance, the better than average direction for this one, and the gloomy atmosphere.

Bela gets to go schizo again, although in *Bowery at Midnight* I think he was aware of his two personalities. In this one, the kindly man he portrays is genuine and he has no memory of the murders he commits.

Joseph H. Lewis adds some nice touches to this one. When Bela is in the anti-social mode, he covers his victim's faces with his coat, maybe so he won't see their expression as he kills them? We have the POV of the victim when Bela drapes the coat over the lens. The film moves along nicely as well. Lewis was also the director of Universal's *Mad Doctor of Market Street* but is best known for directing the noirish film *Gun Crazy.*

On hand as the twin brothers is John McGuire, whose most prominent role was as the lead in the B movie classic, *Stranger on the Third Floor* with Peter Lorre. A forerunner of the film noir genre, *Stranger* almost qualifies as an out and out horror film due to Lorre's presence and a great dream sequence.

Cast as a butler, what else, is respected black actor, Clarence Muse. Fortunately, he avoids the stereotyped performance of the day. He is dignified, well spoken and respected by the household. It is perfectly reasonable for anyone working for Lugosi in this one to think that he is driving on three wheels. Muse was the carriage driver in *White Zombie*, so he should be on a first name basis with Bela by this time.

All in all, one of the better Monograms, and like ALL of the Monograms, a lot of fun.

NIGHT OF THE LIVING DEAD

A group of zombie misfits get together and change forever what a zombie is.

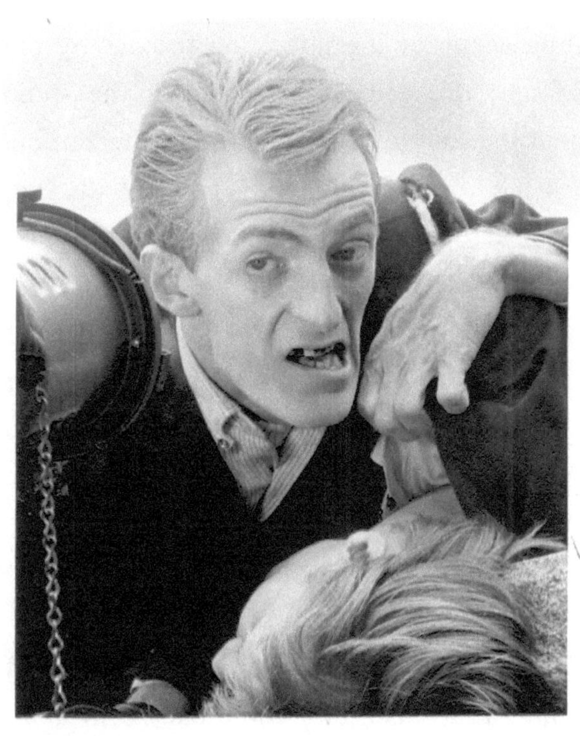

That's right, folks. The zombies of *White Zombie, King of the Zombies, Revenge of the Zombies,* etc, were forever changed by this groundbreaking movie. Gone were the mindless slaves, replaced by flesh eating machines. As much as I admire and respect this movie, the "overkill," if you pardon the expression, of zombie films has reached capacity. How many variations can you do of this type of movie?

George Romero took chunks of money when he could get it and made a low budget classic that went from public and critical revulsion to critical and public adoration.

There's not much I can add to in terms of perspective to this movie. It's been analyzed to death, (can't stop the puns with this movie), and anyone with half a brain, (see what I mean)?, know that it created a brand new sub genre of the horror film, second only to vampire films.

I saw this on some double or triple bill at the drive in when it first came out. I was a teenager and thought I was used to horror films, but I was totally unprepared for this one. I couldn't believe what I was seeing. I was revolted, fascinated, scared to death and sometime amused. Strangely enough, the scariest scene was not a gory one, but the opening scene of the attack on the car by the cemetery zombie. I found this pure up and down the spine chilling. Something about the frantic determination of the zombie to get in that car and kill the woman just paralyzed me with fear. So much so, that later on when we made the feature, The Dungeon of Dr. Dreck, I paid homage to that scene for our opening scene.

After that first viewing, I really didn't know how I felt about the movie. Then I had another crack at it a few years later when it was midnight movie at the local indoor theater. I knew what to expect now, and at this point I started looking at it as a movie instead of a black and white punch in the stomach. The documentary feel to it, the gritty plot and the low budget did the opposite of detract from it, it added to it. To me the later color followups didn't have the same impact, because you were mindful of watching a movie. Funny that black and white can seem more real than color.

The movie is in constant rotation on all horror host shows, and I certainly have shown it myself. For good or bad, it was the turning point in the way we view horror films today.

WHAT MADE THE MOVIE EXTRA UNNERVING WAS BOTH THE BLACK AND WHITE PHOTOGRAPHY, AND THE VERY ORDINARY LOOKING ZOMBIES WALKING AROUND.

JESSE JAMES MEETS FRANKENSTEIN'S DAUGHTER

Actually it's Frankenstein's granddaughter, but what the hell. She is riding the crazy train like her ancestors, so who cares?

What a double feature this was! Yup, saw this in the theater in its initial release along with *Billy the Kid vs Dracula*. What better way to spend a Saturday afternoon when you're thirteen years old?

I recall being disappointed that the monster in this one wasn't too monstrous looking. He was just a big muscle bound guy with a shaved head and a 360 degree stitch on his noggin. In both of these features, Jesse James and Billy the Kid were presented rather sympathetically; I guess you had to have someone to root for, even if it's an outlaw.

You got to hand to Embassy Pictures though, for releasing two features that took the "Abbott and Costello Meet" premise to a new frontier. Add to that the fact that William Beaudine directed both flicks, and it seems like two old wacky Monogram movies with the benefit of color.

And a colorful one this is. Maria Frankenstein even goes to the trouble of painting nice colorful stripes on the life transferring helmut she wears, which has two winglike sidewinders on it that would make Thor jealous. She goes further into B movie land when she renames the transformed cowboy, "Igor." I guess it's an easier name to remember than the cowboy's original name, Hank.

Jim Davis is the sheriff and Nestor Paiva is the saloon keeper which makes this movie even more like a throwback to the fifties.

Of course we have the monster get a crush on the local female, Juanita, which turns him into monster mush by the end of the movie. In a normal western, Jesse James would get his comeuppance at the end, but this time it's the Frankenstein family that takes the fall.   Just sit back and enjoy the weirdness that someone went through the trouble to make just for you!

A word about its co-feature: *Billy the Kid vs Dracula*. I thought this was the better of the two, primarily because they had the sense to make John Carradine play Dracula, unlike the boneheaded

DR. MARIA FRANKENSTEIN IS EXCITED TO WATCH HER FIRST SUPER BOWL GAME ON TV.

movie, *Blood of Dracula's Castle* where he plays the butler instead of the count. Carradine is dressed up more like Svengali, with a top hat, cap, mustache and beard. The Carradine eyes are turned up to "11," and John has a grand time hamming it up. The silliest thing in this one is at the end. After shooting the count to no avail, they throw the gun at him, and it knocks him out! Then they can drive the stake into him. All this time and we didn't know the easiest way to kill Dracula is to throw a blunt object at his head.

THE DEVIL BAT

Lugosi could be called "Batman" in this little gem for PRC.

This is one of the all time best Lugosi movies. It's his only one for PRC, but he walks away with a great part. Dr. Carruthers, has no one to blame but himself, since he sold all the rights to his formula, but Bela being Bela, he thinks he should still get revenge in the most outlandish way possible. His king sized devil bat is actually rather effective as it comes barreling out of the window and zeroes in on people's neck. The most fun aspect is Lugosi's "after shave" he conveniently gives out as samples to his victims. Caution: if you ever see Bela in a supermarket giving out samples, just walk on by. Bela really enjoys saying his "goodbyes" to his soon to be victim, and we laugh along with him. No one he is bumping off is very likable anyway. Bela also pulls off a line only he could. When listening to some clown on the radio talking about the murders, he calls him a "bombastic ignoramus!" I'm still waiting for an opportunity to use this phrase in conversation. The good guy is Dave O'Brien, a mainstay of poverty role films. Usually playing the hero or sidekick, he is perhaps best known to mainstream audiences as the wild eyed drug crazed loon in *Reefer Madness*. Even more fun is Dave's boss in the movie is none other than Elmer Fudd, that is, Arthur Q. Bryan. You know who it is the minute he opens his mouth.

Sometimes I've wondered if Lugosi would have been better off signing with PRC rather than Monogram. Imagine if he had been cast as Zucco's vampire brother in *Dead Men Walk*? Plus, he'd have Dwight Frye as his servant again!

PRC being what it is, (not caring much about continuity between films), later made *Devil Bat's Daughter,* in which Lugosi's character is completely exonerated, even though we saw what he was doing in this picture! You can't fool me, PRC! What do you think I am? A bombastic ignoramus? (Close enough.)

CARNIVAL OF SOULS

Is she dead or alive? Are we even sure about ourselves?

Everyone once in a while, someone turns out a low budget classic. This is one of them.

Fate plays a role both in the plot of this film and of its origin as a movie. Director Herk Harvey drove by a deserted pavilion one day and it struck him how spooky it looked. Thus was the germ of an idea hatched.

Emptiness seems to be a theme of this movie to me. The emptiness of the abandoned tourist resort. The emptiness of the people involved. Candace Hilligoss' character we never get to know before she "died," but her inner life seems as empty as the buildings on that lot. Her sleazy neighbor played by Sidney Berger doesn't seem to have much going on inside him other than trying to score with Candace. Her doctor gives her empty platitudes which don't help her. And when the sound of her world gets temporarily stifled, Hilligoss' world is even emptier.

Harvey's film is a wonder of simplicity. With just the simple makeup effects of white face and dark eyes, he creates a nightmare world of shadow people who can pop up in your mirror, outside your car window, and emerge from underwater as a harbinger of doom. You truly can't cheat death;   your place is always waiting for you.

Hilligoss's only other movie that I know of was in Del Tenny's *Curse of the Living Corpse*, a not little B film itself. I did not see the remake of this nor do I want to. It couldn't possibly capture the otherworldliness of this one.

A movie that got pretty much ignored initially due to bad distribution, it has taken it's rightful place as a modest masterpiece of moody horror; without gore, without CGI, without known stars, it outdoes most modern horror films in weaving it's eerie spell.

"WANT A RIDE ON THE GHOUL BUS?"

HOUSE ON HAUNTED HILL

Vincent Price and William Castle join forces to create one of the most enjoyable haunted house pictures ever.

As a kind of Ying to *The Haunting*'s Yang, *House on Haunted Hill* provides the in your face spook show scares that The Haunting does with subtlety and sound.

I loved this movie the first time I saw it and can watch it endlessly without ever getting tired of it.

Naturally the fact that William Castle directed it and Vincent Price is the star are big factors on the joy scale, but Robb White's script certainly is a big plus, especially in the back and forth acidic banter between Price and co-star, Carol Ohmart. Elisha Cook is always welcome in any film, and his gloomy, doomy Pritchard is a delight. At beddy bye time his uttering of "What's the use of saying good night?" is one of my all time favorite lines in a horror film.

The blind woman caretaker scared the bejeezus out of me when she first appears in that dark room, her hands raised like claws and her dead eyes exuding malevolence. I was a kid when I first saw the film on TV, and I still get a chill when I see it.

I never saw it in the theater with Emergo, but I think this time that Castle didn't need the gimmick. I think the movie stands fine on its own and the skeleton gag floating over the audience would seem a distraction.

Richard Long is a likable leading man, but I wish the leading lady wouldn't panic and scream so much.

Carol Ohmart, also seen in *Spider Baby*, is the perfect, scheming wife, but no match for Vinnie. Who is?

Fun stuff include the bloody head in the suitcase, the clutching hand from the drapes, and my particular favorite, Ohmart's corpse appearing at the window while a rope coils around Carolyn Craigs ankles, (in stop motion, I might add).

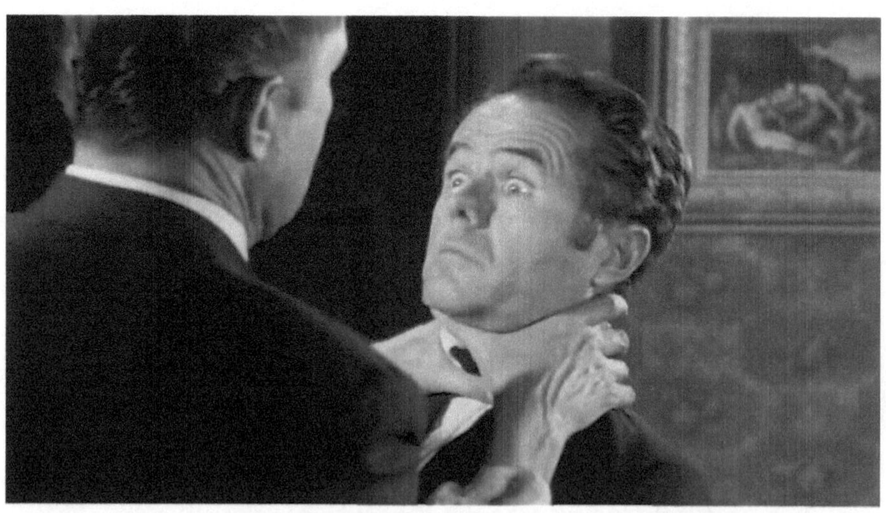

ELISHA COOK SPENT MOST OF HIS MOVIE CAREER BEING ROUGHED UP BY JUST ABOUT EVERYBODY. NICE WORK IF YOU CAN GET IT.

A perfect movie to see on Halloween night as you open your seventh bar of snack size Snickers.

Many would site *The Tingler* as their favorite Castle movie, but for me it's this one. I love *The Tingler*, too, but this movie is one of my fondest childhood memories and is still a damn fun movie.

CITY OF THE DEAD

Witches run wild in an old New England town and it's not even spring break.

I remember seeing this one in the old days of the UHF station boom. That sounds strange to write in these days of cable, although antenna TV is making a big comeback. The UHF antenna was a wire loop in the back of the set and it had limited twisting ability. The UHF stations didn't have powerful signals back then in the 60's, so the best you could hope for a picture low on "snow" and it was a big bonus if you didn't get a ghost image. Oldsters know what I'm talking about. Under those conditions, the movie didn't have a big impact on me then. I knew Christopher Lee, but because he wasn't some kind of recognizable monster, I may have been disappointed.

However, years later when it came out on DVD, I finally got to see the clean and mean version of the film and it jumped up in my estimation considerably.

Again we have a movie with little special effects to speak of, unless you consider a fog machine a special effect. It's the camera angles, the stark black and white photography and the underlying creepiness of the town that get to you. When the doomed woman at the beginning walks through town at night and the inhabitants turn to stare at her, shot from a low angle with shadows playing against their craggy faces, you know that this town could never be a tourist attraction. Their welcome mat would be made of quicksand.

The movie predates *Psycho* in the surprise turn of events at the beginning. The woman who you expect to be the lead gets bumped off, leaving you to set your sights on another character to guide you through this.

Lee himself is, as always, a formidable figure. First as the college professor, and even more so later by being a leader of the witches cult. He is matched by Patricia Jessel, the owner of the

local hotel, which is parked conveniently over an underground meeting place for the evil folk. Another stand out is Valentine Dyall as one of the long lived witches. His sepulchral voice has graced many a Brit film, and if there was ever a voice of doom, it's his voice.

The director, John Llewellyn Moxey, does a fantastic job with this movie, as he would years later when he helmed one of the greatest TV movies of all time, *The Night Stalker*.

Yet another one of our Halloween shows, sure to give you the chills in between throwing candy to trick or treaters.

BOWERY AT MIDNIGHT

Bela does double duty as a respectable professor by day and a sociopathic criminal by night. Hey, everyone needs a hobby.

Bela gets another workout courtesy of Monogram pictures. And what a pickle he's in this time, although he asked for it.

As a criminal mastermind during the night hours, he chooses bad company. Knowing Tom Neal in real life was hazardous enough, but Bela makes Tom his accomplice in this flick. That can't be good. Especially when another member of his gang is a whacked out doctor that says he can raise the dead. The guys that have been knocked off from Bela's crime hobby are buried in the basement, so the potential is there for a zombie movie. But that doesn't happen. (The closest Bela ever gets to zombies is in the comedy/horror flick *Zombies on Broadway*.)

The script to this movie seems like four different writers were taking turns writing a page without paying any attention to what the other writers wrote. (Say THAT three times fast.) It's a crime thriller! It's a science fiction movie! It's a zombie movie! It's a crime thriller! It's a melodrama! It's Monogram, is what it is, so you don't need to figure out the plot, you just let it happen, like a tire with a slow leak.

It would seem that Lugosi loves his wife and may be making that extra dirty money on her behalf, but since he knocks her off later, I guess that wasn't it. He should have paid more attention to the kooky doctors' claim of reanimating the dead. There's a cash cow if there ever was one. Actually, SOMEBODY should have paid attention to the doc's formula, because the hero of the piece, played by John Archer, gets killed, and then is revitalized by the formula and is perfectly normal at the end. Nobody seems to think that's a big deal. These guys would probably never think personal computers would become a big thing, either.

"YES, YOUR HEAD WOULD LOOK GREAT OVER MY MANTLEPIECE.".

At any rate, we see the living dead for about five-seconds at the end, when Bela gets positive proof that the doctor meant what he said. I wonder if Bela's character thought, "Damn! I should have listened to that crackpot!" as he was being torn to shreds by vengeful cadavers.

One little sidelight is when we get a glimpse of Lou Costello's brother, Pat, in a cameo as a bum. He looks and sounds like Lou, which makes you wish he was in it more to add some comedy to the this movie.

THE TERROR

Roger Corman must be part Native American. He never wastes any part of the animal.   In this case, he never wastes standing sets with Karloff hanging around.

It must be fun to write scenes for a movie when you have no idea of what the plot is. That's what supposedly happened here, as Karloff's scenes were written and shot posthaste, and then left to others to write some kind of plot around them. It went that way with directors as well, as everyone seemed to have a hand in directing this: Roger Corman, Francis Ford Coppola, Monte Hellman, Jack Nicholson, Jack Hill, Gumby, etc.

We also get the bonus of having both Jonathan Haze and Dick Miller in the same movie again, although they have little or no interaction.

Jack Nicholson just doesn't look right in a period piece; he was okay in The Raven, because it was a comedy, but here, he's hard to believe. But we can cut him some slack. It was early in his career and he hadn't found his niche yet. The sets are certainly impressive, and Karloff's scenes are what really make the movie. It just doesn't make a whole lot of sense, especially the ending. I still don't know why the leading lady, played by Sandra Knight, turns to melted chocolate at the end. I saw this in the theater and thought the effect was cool, but I didn't get it then or now. Did the spirit of Karloff's wife possess this girl? Why does she rot away when the real corpse was in the coffin already living in decay city? I felt sorry for Boris having to get drenched in the large pool of water at the end, remembering his back problems and ill health. Being the trooper he was, he put up with it, but I can't help but think it hastened his demise.

THE ORIGINAL ODD COUPLE.

It's Bela Lugosi in living color! Sort of.

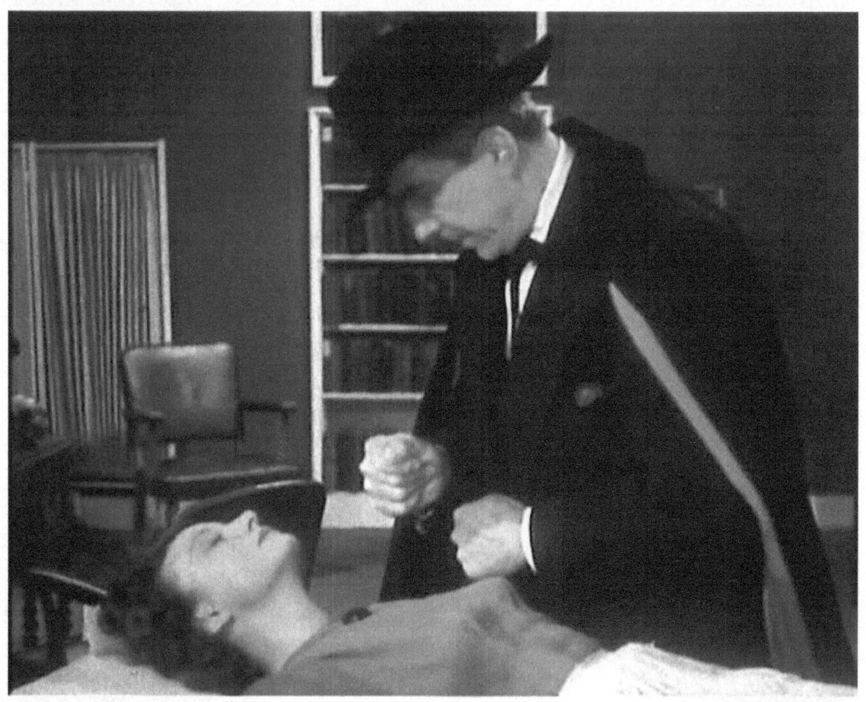

A movie narrated by a corpse? No, it's not *Sunset Boulevard*, but this obscure cheapie, shot in an old color process. The color is kind of comic book like, but that's just right for this movie.

You may think it's a Monogram at first sight. There's Bela, there's George Zucco, there's Angelo Rossitto! It's the color that tells you it's definitely not Monogram.

It seems older than it is, due to the outlandish melodrama of the plot, but that's okay with me. If it's a B movie, that means it'll be short.

I've heard that Bela requested Angelo Rossitto to be with him in this picture, because he considered him a good luck charm. Whether that's true or not, I don't know, but Angelo was happy to get work, seeing as his personal circumstances limited his casting possibilities. Lugosi seems much more comic in this one, on purpose, as he's there strictly as a red herring, and pretty obvious one at that. He's dressed like Dracula, plus he's a hypnotist too.

Nat Pendleton plays his usual big dumb guy role, and he's joined by Joyce Compton, who usually played dim witted kewpie doll roles. George Zucco, alas, is gone quite quickly. It would have been even more fun if he stuck around.

I saw this on TV when I was very little. It's so embedded in my mind I can still remember what channel I saw it on; Channel 10  out of Providence, RI. The reason it traumatized me was early on in the movie, when they open the box and show the dummy head of the woman. Those wild staring eyes haunted me for years. Even looking at the photo now gives me the creeps. I wouldn't be able to sleep at night if I had that head propped up on my bedroom bureau staring at me. Brrrrr! I had that fear about wide staring eyes. I remember I was freaked out for years from the beginning scenes of Voodoo Island, which starred Karloff. I saw it at the drive in and the zombie like guy at the beginning of the movie with his staring eyes just gave me nightmares. Also the poster from *Children of the Damned* had the same effect on me.

I didn't see this for a very long time in the color version until around the 1980s. I remember seeing it on the Nashville station which featured the Phantom of the Opry as the horror host. I thank him for my first glimpse of the color version of this one!

THE BRAIN EATERS

Creatures attach themselves to the backs of people and control their every move. Much like being married.

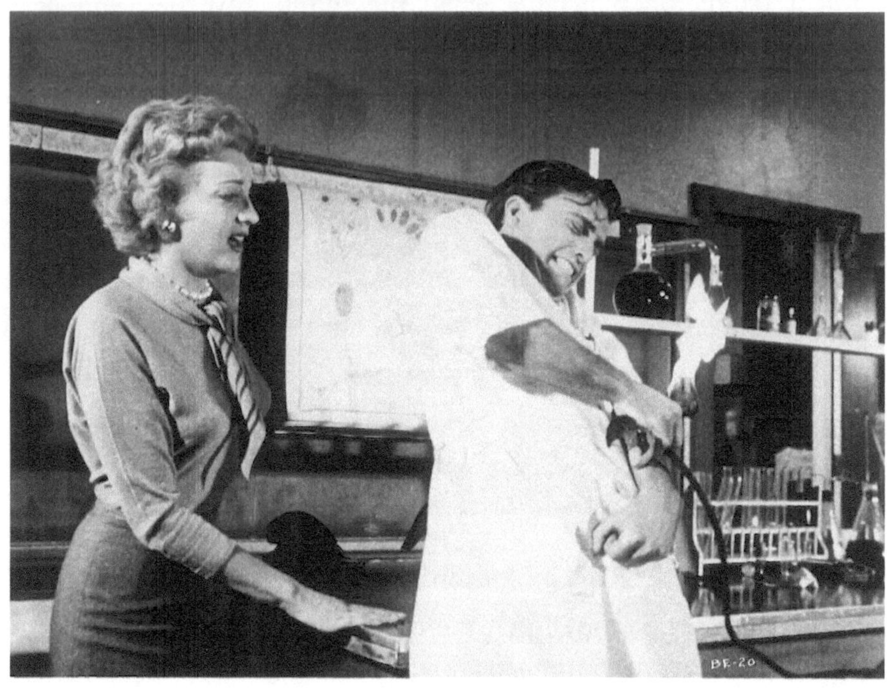

This movie's main claim to fame is the cameo by Leonard Nimoy at the end. He plays the old guy sitting in a foggy part of the spaceship. We can't make out his face really, but there's no mistaking the voice.I saw the trailer for this movie at the drive in. (See how much I was at the drive in during my checkered youth?) The brain eaters looked like little moving hamburgers to me at the time. I later found out that they were windup ladybug toys, covered with fur and pipe cleaners. I actually had one of those ladybug toys when I was little, not aware that I was holding a brain eater in my hand! So call me hopeless, but I applaud the ingenuity of making those little critters out of whatever they could find. People with no money have to be clever and resourceful. With Ed Nelson producing and Bruno VeSoto directing, we have a different looking AIP movie. Here's a movie that I think gets unfairly trashed. Yes, it's cheap and the plot was ripped off from Robert Heinlein's *The Puppet Masters*, but VeSoto directs in a noirish style and incorporates some unusual angles into it which makes it more than a by the numbers monster movie. Even though it's a lump on the back underneath the clothing, you can almost feel those things pulsating on your own back. A similar plot was unraveled on the Outer Limits series in an episode called The Invisibles. In that one George McCready was the evil master, and it's too bad they couldn't have stuck him in this movie to increase the creepy factor.

I also like that these invaders come from inner earth, and instead of a spaceship, they have a drill like cone jutting out of the ground.

LEONARD NIMOY BEFORE HE QUIT SMOKING.

If you're claustrophobic like I am, I also get queasy when Ed Nelson has to crawl through the narrow tunnels into the vessel.

Give this movie a fair look, and you may just like it.

THE DEATH KISS

The Dracula cast without Dracula. Too bad.

Yes, Bela Lugosi, David Manners and Edward Van Sloan are in this obscure mystery from 1932. Just a year after Dracula they appeared in this independent film from KBS Studios.

A murder occurs on a movie set and everyone is under suspicion, otherwise this would be a very short movie. It might have been odd for audiences to see Lugosi so soon after Dracula, acting like a normal guy. David Manners is also quite different from the usual feckless hero he was in other films, portraying a more lively smart aleck. Van Sloan is a movie director in this one, so it's a change from being the all wise poobah he usually played in the Universal classics. I've seen Van Sloan as a villain twice in films, one being *Behind the Mask*, (with Karloff!), and in a low budget mystery, *Murder on the Campus*.

A unique feature if you can find a print of it, is that sometimes hand colored frames will appear. I've seen them in the version I have; gunshot flashes, projection room light and a few other places are briefly illuminated with a mix of orange and yellow. Kind of cool for an old film.

If you're looking for a horror film you'll be disappointed, but it's still fun to see these guys mixing it up again. Too bad Dwight Frye isn't in it.

"I SAT THIS ONE OUT."

234

THE CREEPER

No, not good old Rondo, but good old Onslow.

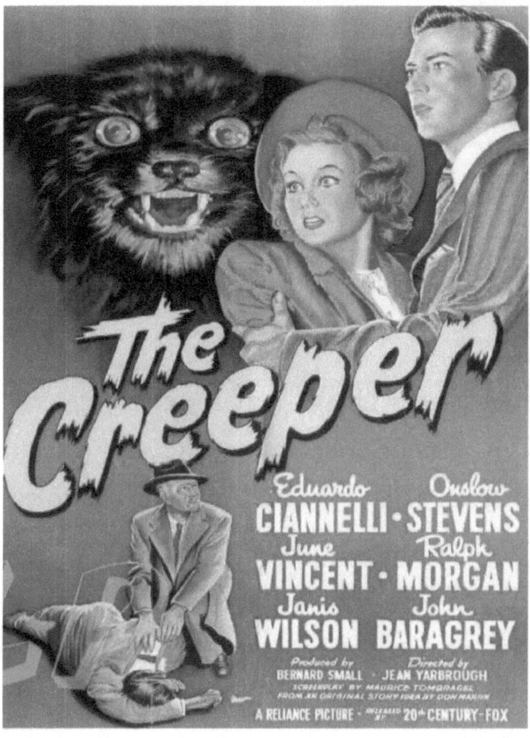

Two old hands at B moviedom, Onslow Stevens and Ralph Morgan appear in this independent production which looks like a Universal movie. The two are scientists experimenting with a process to illuminate human organs for medical research. The strange story evolves into a mystery involving Morgan's daughter, and the terrifying nightmares she keeps having about a cat creature.

You know how the big Pharma commercials give you that long list of side effects that may or may not kill you? Well, let's just say the side effects of this experiment will make you scratch the furniture and chase mice.

Quite a moody little number with a rather unique plot. It's finding these little diamonds in the rough that make life worth living for weirdos like me.

Onslow Stevens is best known for his own take as a mad scientist in *House of Dracula*. Sure, he starts out as a humanitarian,

but John Carradine's' Dracula louses up his experiment and turns him into a pseudo vampire via a blood transfusion. Stevens was all over the map in his career, usually playing small supporting roles. He can seen in the mystery, *Secret of the Blue Room, Them!* and many other thrillers. He did have the lead in an unusual serial, *The Vanishing Shadow.*

Ralph Morgan was a busy man, both in serials like *Gangbusters* and cheap B's like T*he Monster Maker*. He could comfortably play both sides of the fence in turns of good and evil. He was Dick Tracy's nemesis in the serial *Dick Tracy VS Crime Inc.* His most memorable performance in my opinion is in *Night Monster*.

This movie could easily be mistaken for a Rondo Hatton movie by its title. Poor Rondo had gone to Creeper heaven by 1948. His last film was *The Brute Man*, originally a Universal production which they palmed off to PRC when Hatton died.

UNKNOWN ISLAND

Richard Denning faces off with some lethargic dinosaurs.

What would we do without the word "unknown" for horror movies? *Unknown Terror, Creeping Unknown, Giant from the Unknown, The Unknown, Land Unknown, X the Unknown, Unknown World;* well, you get the idea.

Richard Denning starts off as a souse in this one, but his presence is valuable as to finding an island where dinosaurs still thrive. He sobers up for the adventure with co-star Virginia Grey, (*House of Horrors*). Unfortunately the captain of the ship they hire is both an alcoholic and is given to spells of insanity from malaria. Filling that bill is Barton McLane, a very familiar face in moviedom appearing in everything from *The Mummy's Ghost* to *The Maltese Falcon.* He rarely played a nice guy and he is in his element here.

The Dinos are the rubber suited kind, and they had to be optically doubled on film since there were too few suits. An 80 year old person could easily outrun them, and they look like they're about to fall over half the time.

The movie was shot in that odd color process called Cinecolor, which kind of has a cartoonish look to it, but I don't find it unpleasant.

I don't think I've ever seen a B movie with Richard Denning in it that I didn't like. *The Day the World Ended, Creature with the Atom Brain, Creature from the Black Lagoon, The Black Scorpion, Target Earth*…I mean who wouldn't want to see these just based on the titles?

I first saw this as a little kid and like most little boys enjoyed seeing anything with dinosaurs in it. Of course the effects are disappointing now, but it's still fun to watch.

IT'S A BEAUTIFUL DAY IN THE
NEIGHBORHOOD…

CAPE CANAVERAL MONSTERS

Two invisible aliens possess a couple of cadavers and try to foul up the entire U.S. space program by themselves. Talk about ambitious.

Phil Tucker, who gave the world *Robot Monster,* is back with a somewhat more straight forward but far less hilarious sci fi cheapie.

Shades of *Invisible Invaders*! Those freeloading aliens are using our nice fresh corpses to create havoc. Quite gruesome for the time, the couple killed in the car crash are scarred and bloody, with the man losing his arm. When they find a cave to hideout in, his severed arm is grafted back on, but doggone it, he is attacked by a guard dog who rips the arm off again. The two walking corpses are played by Jason Johnson and Katherine Victor. Johnson is one of those familiar character actors you see everywhere in movies and TV, but his role in this movie is substantial and he really gives a pretty creepy performance. Victor is one of the poor victims of Jerry Warren films, (*Teenage Zombies, Wild World of Batwoman*), but I can say this movie is a step up for her. The aliens have run-ins with some teenagers which was common during this era. Later some poor slob is kidnapped and involuntarily donates his arm to the male alien. Maybe the second arm is the charm. These aliens have a problem in that the corpses keep rotting, which is one of the many odd touches this movie has.

The movie went straight to television instead of a theatrical release. I saw it late one night and it didn't impress me one way or the other at the time. I did play it on my show, *The Dungeon of Dr. Dreck*, and now I kind of enjoy its sleazy, cheesy charm. And it has a downer ending, another unusual touch.

"YOU NEED A FACE LIFT. YOUR CHIN IS ALMOST HITTING THE FLOOR."

LONG HAIR OF DEATH

Barbara Steele steals my heart again as a witch's descendent who is twitching for revenge.

Barbara Steele, whose exotic beauty enlivened many an Italian horror film, plays two parts in this story of vengeance. Her first role as Helen is the daughter of a woman accused and executed for witchcraft. The dirtbag royalty who condemned her is confronted by Helen so he kills her. Nice to be royalty, isn't it? Later on a mysterious woman named Mary, (Barbara Steele, again), shows up to exact revenge. The ending may remind some of the conclusion of the movie, *The Wicker Man.*

Like a lot of the Italian horror films, this one is pretty slow moving, with the characters aimlessly wandering around through castle hallways and dungeons to pad the time out. The story is good enough, but the lackadaisical treatment of it bogs it down. I confess when I showed it on my program, I did some extensive editing of the movie to speed things up and it improved it immensely. If you want to see the whole thing, you can find it online.

THE SPIDERWOMAN STRIKES BACK

Nothing like knocking off people left and right without drawing attention to yourself.

Double your fun with Rondo Hatton and Gale Sondergaard as a nefarious duo playing with spider venom.

Sondergaarde plays Zenobia Dollard, a blind but rich woman who hires young secretaries to look after her. Her man servant is Mario, played by Rondo Hatton, who mercifully doesn't speak in this film. Brenda Joyce plays Jean Kingsley, one of a long line of secretaries for Zenobia. Seems like the poor things keep "disappearing" and Zenobia has to recruit some new victim. Zenobia, who really isn't blind, is mixing the blood of her former secretaries with spider venom. I guess she thinks a death serum will be a big seller on the open market.

Rondo is effective as the silent servant, as the poor guy skulks around the house taking orders from his nasty boss. Rondo never

could handle dialog without sounding funny, as evidenced by his speaking role in Universal's *House of Horrors*.

Adding to the fun is the hero of the piece, none other than Sky King! Yes, it's Kirby Grant, known to us 50's kids as the flying hero of that series.

Although both roles were played by Sondergaard, it should be noted that the Spider Woman in this movie is no relation to the same villain in the Sherlock Holmes movie *The Spider Woman*.

NIGHT OF TERROR

Bela Lugosi in one of his earliest red herring roles.

When I was a kid, our second go to station for horror films was channel 12 in Providence. On Friday nights they ran *Chiller*, which would run two to three movies in a row starting at 11:30. It was there I saw my first Todd Slaughter film, *Face at the Window, Horrors of the Black Museum* and this obscure Columbia film.

A maniac killer is on the loose! He is seen running around in his black coat and hat and his long knife, killing people indiscriminately. How else would a maniac kill? Arthur Hornsby, played by George Meeker. proclaims that he has developed a serum whereby a person can go without oxygen for a certain amount of time. He proves it by having himself buried alive to be dug up later at a predetermined time. When he does come out of the dirt, he finds that his rich as dirt uncle has been killed by the maniac! Now he inherits the fortune! What a coincidence!

Bela plays Degar, a combo butler and mystic who spends his time looking ominous. To make him even more untrustworthy, he wears a turban! Heavens to Betsy!

Wallace Ford, who excelled at playing fast talking newspaper men walks around the mansion like he owns it, but he does come in handy at the end. Unfortunately, the stereotyped black butler is a particularly egregious example of the institutionalized racism of this era.

The end is hilarious and inspired a character for our show. After he has been dispatched, the Maniac gets up off the floor, walks to the camera and threatens the audience not to reveal the ending to anyone or he'll haunt you! Going by his looks the audience may have kept their collective mouths shut just on the off chance that he may just do that.

"WILL YOU GET OFF THE PHONE? I'M EXPECTING A CALL FROM MY LAWYER!"

THE CRAWLING HAND

Here's your chance to hear the original "Bird is the Word" by the Rivingtons!

I saw the trailer for this one at the drive in and the scariest part for me was the infected astronaut on the TV screen. The black rings around his eyes, his sweaty face and unsettling voice really spooked me. I thought about that face for years after that. I finally got to see the movie on TV and that guy still got to me.

This movie is chock full of familiar faces. Kent Taylor, Peter Breck, Allison Hayes, Rod Lauren and the Skipper himself, Alan Hale, Jr.

After the ghoulish looking astronaut is killed when his spaceship crashes, his severed arm begins not only to crawl around on its own, but it can infect people with the same bug nutty disease the astronaut had. Rod Lauren's character lucks out and gets infected, and he periodically succumbs to it, developing the same black rings around his eyes and becoming ever so slightly homicidal.

The most effective scene is in a diner where he attacks the owner one night. In their struggle they hit the old juke box, and the Rivington's tune, "Bird is the Word" plays throughout the sequence. It's a jarring contrast to the action which makes it even more creepy.

The arm monster works pretty well. I mean, we know it's a real guy's arm most of the time, just out of camera range, but it helps it's a long arm and not just the stump of the wrist. It's also pretty messed up to add to the creepiness of it.

The whole movie has a sleazy atmosphere, but hell, I like that. Allison Hayes is wasted in her role, but we get to see more of Taylor, Breck and Hale. And by the end of the movie, you'll appreciate what great public minded citizens cats are.

"I'LL BET YOU ANY AMOUNT OF MONEY THAT GILLIGAN IS BEHIND ALL THIS TROUBLE!"

GIGANTIS, THE FIRE MONSTER

Godzilla moonlights under another name.

Godzilla Raids Again was the sequel to the original Godzilla, produced by Toho Productions of Japan. We all know that the original big G was destroyed in the first one, so it turns out there was another one kept on ice until he was needed.

The plan was for the original American team that reshot Godzilla to do the same thing with the sequel. It was to be called the *Volcano Monsters*, and new scenes were intended to be shot for the American version. However, they decided to dub the movie instead. Then they changed Godzilla's name to Gigantis, seemingly thinking that the public might be confused since the first Godzilla was killed. Keye Luke, Paul Frees and believe or not, *Star Trek*'s George Takei were the prime voices.

Of course, with the dubbing came the awkward translation. To this day, I've heard no one say someone was full of "banana oil" as an insult. Gigantis's sparing partner is Anguirus, a kind of turtle like Dino who doesn't fare well against Gigantis in their battle. The city of Tokyo also doesn't fare well, as everything gets royal destroyed by the disagreeable titans.

In the finale, Gigantis is put to rest by airplanes bombing the frosty mountains around him so he gets covered in ice from which he can't escape. That is until *King Kong VS Godzilla*, when Gigantis comes out of the ice and remembers who he really is.

DEVIL BAT'S DAUGHTER

The evil Dr. Carruthers gets vindicated in this cockeyed sequel to the Devil Bat.

Remember Bela Lugosi as Dr. Carruthers? Remember how he created a giant bat that would dive bomb his enemies and kill them? Well, your memory is wrong. Dr. Carruthers was a great guy, according to this movie which completely upends the previous movie.

Rosemary La Planche plays Nina, the troubled daughter of the late unlamented Dr. Carruthers. She's not aware of it at first, until she is found in a trance at the old Carruthers place. With help of a psychiatrist, a Dr. Elliot, she finds that she is indeed the daughter of Carrauthers, who had previously been considered a vampire. Since Carruthers was not married in the original, you have to wonder where she came from. When Dr. Elliot's wife is brutally murdered, all eyes turn to her. However, it turns out there's a dire plot to frame her for the murder of the shrink's wife. With the use of drugs, Elliot was getting Nina to believe she was taking after her father and turning into a murderess. But wait! Dr. Carruthers diary is found and it turns out he is innocent. His bats simply escaped from his lab, killed some people and eventually killed him. The real bad guy, Dr. Elliot, is shot by police when he tries to escape after being unmasked.

It's best to just plain forget the plot of *The Devil Bat* in order to get any enjoyment out of this film. PRC, the producing studio, apparently thought people either didn't care or never saw the first movie. It actually would have been a much better film if she really was a crazy murderer instead of the victim of a big frame up. It should be noted that it is Dr. Carruther's diary that they base their assumption of his innocence on. Sure, Carruthers could write in his own diary what a poor, misunderstood and most of all, INNOCENT genius he was.

"SEE? I TOLD YOU I VAS INNOCENT!"

A pretty dull and plodding movie whose main point of interest is that the star, Rosemary La Planche was the star of *Strangler of the Swamp,* and the director of that movie and this one is Frank Wisbar. Wisbar did much better work with Strangler, but then again he didn't have this cockamamie script to work with.

QUEEN OF BLOOD

See what happens when you pick up strangers?

Roger Corman went out and bought some Russian science fiction films that contained really impressive special effects. Using and reusing them, he was able to cobble together three different movies: *Queen of Blood, Voyage to a Prehistoric Planet* and *Voyage to the Planet of Prehistoric Women. Queen of Blood* is definitely the best of the lot.

Directed by Curtis Harrington, the film has a fun cast that includes Basil Rathbone, John Saxon and Dennis Hopper. The most striking cast member is Florence Marley.

The Russian footage is nicely integrated into the whole, as our intrepid crew of space pilots fly to rescue an alien ship which crashed on Mars. The ship was supposedly sending an ambassador to Earth before the accident. The astronauts recover an alien woman and bring her on board. Big mistake. This alien dame is akin to a bloodsucking insect and she wastes no time draining the crew of their red stuff. Forrest J Ackerman of *Famous Monsters Magazine* has a funny cameo at the end.

Dennis Hopper doesn't last long. He looks like he did in the movie *Night Tide*. From this movie you could never imagine him turning into Frank Booth in David Lynch's *Blue Velvet*. John Saxon is his usually stoic self, but it is Marley, whom without saying a word, steals the show. Her unique makeup and look is definitely chilling, especially when she nails you with her mesmerizing eyes. Rathbone has a decent supporting role. He also showed up in *Voyage to the Prehistoric Planet*, but his role here is more substantial.

Catch this one if you can. It's like one of those pulp stories in old magazines.

"I KNOW THAT GUY! THAT'S FORRY ACKERMAN!"

FRANKENSTEIN MEETS THE SPACE MONSTER

Mary Shelley is spinning in her grave.

In all seriousness, this movie was meant to be anything but serious. They must have had several tongues in cheek when they made this one.

Larry Buchanan, a famous maker of cheap science fiction movies for television, was beaten to the punch with this movie, as the theme of this movie is *Mars Needs Women*! Naturally they come to Earth to start nabbing nubile young women in bikinis to take back with them. Princess Marcuzon is the leader and she is assisted by Nadir, an effeminate Mr. Spock type who has some of the funniest lines.

Where's Frankenstein? The best they could do is have an astronaut android made from different body parts that gets shot down by the wacky Martians. The android is called Frank, and after he crashes, half of his face is turned into burnt pizza and his

255

brain is all out of kilter. He eventually does battle with the space monster of the title, a mutant the aliens brought with them just for laughs. The space monster actually looks like a Larry Buchanan monster; no, it looks better than any Larry Buchanan monster.

The only recognizable actor in this is James Karen, who later starred in the cult favorite *Return of the Living Dead* and the big deal production, *Poltergeist.*

The movie is padded with some really lame songs. I'll admit when I showed it on my program I edited them out to fit a time slot. It's still a jaw dropping movie to watch if you haven't seen it.

THE DUNGEON GANG

Moaner Johnson(Lorna Nogueira) was my sidekick for many years, but she had to step away from the role. She was a fan favorite and I miss the character. However, Lorna still appears in other roles just to keep her hand in.

Madame Nicotina, (Roberta Marsden) is a psychic, (so she says), and has been on the show since its first season. She claims to have gotten her psychic powers from being hit by a tobacco truck, but I think she's just blowing smoke, if you know what I mean. Her sidekick is poor Shrunken Ed. Ed was a whole person at one time, but when he was having mental problems, he decided to go to a head shrinker. He went to the wrong kind, lost his body and had his head somewhat reduced before he knew what hit him.

Groaner Johnson, (Diane Mela), is a zombie. She is a conniving, greedy zombie most of the time, which is why she never gets invited to any parties. She does run the concession stand during our drive in episodes, though, which shows some responsibility on her part, but the stuff she sells is really inedible.

Uncle Mess, (Dwight Kemper) is sure a mess. He's Moaner and Groaner's uncle, and he died some time ago but refused to accept it. He is also one of the most inept inventors I've ever known, and that's saying a lot.

Stu B. Rat and Williard P. Gnaw are our house rats. Unfortunately they both can talk and they certainly behave like rats whenever they can.

They are popular in their mini series of Space Rats.

Michael Legge, aka Dr. Dreck, is a has been; I mean, he HAS BEEN a horror host on The Dungeon of Dr. Dreck for over a decade. The show currently plays on many national public access stations courtesy of PEG Media.

Along with his lovely co-host, Moaner, and various other co-hosts, he shows a huge variety of public domain movies in the horror, science fiction and mystery genres. He genuinely loves the movies he shows, warts and all, and is more likely to defend their shortcomings than attack them.

Michael Legge is also a prolific underground/no budget film maker. His company, Sideshow Cinema, has many feature films available at various web outlets. Dr. Dreck himself has made two appearances with Sideshow Cinema; Dungeon of Dr. Dreck, the movie, and as a short film, Who Stole Shrunken Ed?

His other films include Monochromia, Braindrainer, My Mouth Lies Screaming, The Brothers Dim, Democrazy, Honey Glaze, Evan Straw and many others.

He resides in Mendon, Massachusetts with his current cat, Cotton.